Dorothea Ruggles-Brise

Traditional Tunes

A collection of ballad airs, chiefly obtained in Yorkshire and the south of Scotland;

together with their appropriate words from broadsides and from oral tradition

Dorothea Ruggles-Brise

Traditional Tunes
A collection of ballad airs, chiefly obtained in Yorkshire and the south of Scotland; together with their appropriate words from broadsides and from oral tradition

ISBN/EAN: 9783744781695

Printed in Europe, USA, Canada, Australia, Japan

Cover: Foto ©Thomas Meinert / pixelio.de

More available books at **www.hansebooks.com**

TRADITIONAL TUNES

A

Collection of Ballad Airs,

CHIEFLY OBTAINED IN YORKSHIRE AND THE
SOUTH OF SCOTLAND;
TOGETHER WITH THEIR APPROPRIATE WORDS
FROM BROADSIDES AND FROM ORAL TRADITION

COLLECTED AND EDITED WITH ILLUSTRATIVE NOTES, BY

FRANK KIDSON.

Oxford:

CHAS. TAPHOUSE & SON, 3, MAGDALEN STREET.

1891.

PREFACE.

WHATEVER may be esteemed the value of the present work, it is the outcome of much pleasant labour.

The compiler's wish has been to at least temporarily rescue from oblivion some few of the old airs, which, passing from mouth to mouth for generations, are fast disappearing before the modern effusions of the music hall and concert room. He believes that many of the airs here noted down are excellent specimens of melody, and as such, are worthy of preservation ; that they have a peculiar quaintness, a sweetness, and a tenderness of expression, absent in the music of the present day, which it is impossible to successfully imitate.

He has endeavoured to set down the airs as far as musical notes will permit with the utmost fidelity, scrupulously avoiding any attempt at arrangement or emendation, for, however desirable it might be in some instances to amend the airs from corruptions which have crept in, the Editor has considered that he would be scarcely justified in tampering with them, as such an attempt at revisal would greatly detract from the antiquarian value of the whole.

It is possible that some musical reader may find much to criticise in the technical arrangement of the melodies. The Editor certainly does not claim that they are absolutely perfect, but he would merely remind such reader of the fact (so well-known to persons who have attempted the feat), that very great difficulty attends the notation of irregular old melodies from untutored singers.

An endeavour to be scrupulously exact in attempting to put the airs before the reader as the Editor has heard them sung, may have led him into some technical errors, but he trusts that these are not serious and will be pardoned.

With regard to the printing of the airs pure and simple and without harmony, an extract from the preface of John Hullah's *Song Book* applies so exactly to the present case that it may be quoted :

"The presentation of these songs without accompaniment has been dictated, not merely by want of space but by the desire to present them in their original forms ; for, in almost every case, the tune is the *only* original part of the music of a national song, the addition even of a bass having been generally made by a later hand—not always guided by a sympathetic spirit."

To the above may be added that the traditional airs forming the present volume have perhaps *never* been harmonized. They have either been sung by a single singer (or by parties of singers in unison), or performed on such a simple instrument as the flute or fiddle. Is it, then, desirable to put such old wine into new bottles?

Where it is, however, deemed desirable to add harmony for the purpose of playing them on the piano, it will be in general found that a thin bass will be more in the character of the old harmonies, put to songs which were printed and issued when these traditional airs were most popular.

The Editor has here to thank the many kind friends who have interested themselves in the work, and to the contributors of airs and songs his warmest acknowledgments are offered. Chief among the contributors to be thanked are Mr. Benjamin Holgate, of Headingley, and Mr. Charles Lolley, of Leeds, to both of whose retentive memories of songs heard in earlier years much of the contents of this book is due.

Mr. Holgate's remembrances are of the songs once popular in and around Leeds, and Mr. Lolley's are of those in the district of Howden, in the East Riding of Yorkshire. Mr. Lolley has, besides, while this work has been in progress, taken a great deal of trouble in collecting airs for it from other parts of the East Riding.

The other contributors are not less warmly thanked, and their contributions acknowledged in the body of the book. To all of these the Editor is greatly obliged, and tenders his heartiest thanks for the patience with which they have in many cases repeated the air until correctly noted down.

The Editor believes that all the airs here set down (with the exception of two or three which he has himself contributed to the *Leeds Mercury Weekly Supplement*), are now printed for the first time. In this belief he may perhaps, in some instances, be mistaken ; he however has made diligent search among early collections, and for reasons, which he gives in the introduction, he feels sure that this class of melody is purely traditional.

In conclusion, he wishes to ask any person who is possessed of, or who can obtain, traditional melodies, to transmit copies to him, as he intends, should circumstances warrant, to issue a second series of this work. He can assure intending contributors that such will be greatly esteemed and duly acknowledged.

128, BURLEY ROAD,

   LEEDS.

CONTENTS.

INTRODUCTION.

When I travelled I took particular delight in hearing the songs and fables that are come down from father to son, and are most in vogue among the common people of the countries through which I passed ; for it is impossible that anything should be universally tasted and approved of by a multitude, though they are only the rabble of the nation, which hath not in it some peculiar aptness to please and gratify the mind of man.—*Spectator, No. 70.*

. . . . . An ordinary song or ballad that is the delight of the common people cannot fail to please all such readers as are not un-qualified for the entertainment by their affectation or ignorance.—*Ibid.*

IF an excuse were necessary for the collection of traditional folk-song, the above sentiments from the pen of such an honoured writer as Joseph Addison would be a sufficient plea. It is to be hoped, however, that the reader of this work has enough sympathy with its design as to render such a one unnecessary. The important part that songs and tunes have played in political history has proved their power in the land and is well-known ; a lengthy list of the ballads which have helped to "make history" in our own country alone could be given were it necessary. Upon some occasions, a foolish song becomes ennobled by the part it plays. In modern days the American anti-slavery hymn, "John Brown's body lies a-mouldering in the Grave," in which there is no rhyme, and certainly no reason, is one which may be quoted.

Dr. Russell in one of his letters from the Crimea gives us a rather pathetic picture of our poor fellows lying cold and miserable in the trenches, knowing that the next day's fight would bring death and wounds to hundreds, solacing themselves by singing familiar songs, and talking of far off England. One of them, a sergeant, struck up the plaintive song, " Annie Laurie," which was gradually taken up by the entire line till hundreds of voices joined in the song. Who would dare to say that the remembrance of the song sung by the loved ones at home would not spur the men to greater daring ?

The collection of songs here given, however, claims nothing heroic in association. They are simply homely ditties, such as were sung by the humbler classes in England round the fireside of farm kitchens or at the plough tail, and the little wit or brilliancy they may possess must not be judged by a very high standard. They were sufficient to interest the original singers, the themes being in most cases familiar subjects. This class of song is fast disappearing before the modern productions, and any young ploughboy who should sing the songs his father or grandfather sung, would be laughed to scorn. Before easy means of transit existed, the songs of a country side remained unaltered for a great length of time, and people delighted to sing the songs which were venerable with age. Now, however, cheap trips to the larger towns enable the country lad to compete with the town's boy in his knowledge of popular musical favourites.

The old traditional songs are fast dying out, never to be recalled. They are now seldom or never sung, but rather *remembered*, by old people. I have found in the course of my search how quickly this class of old airs is disappearing, for I have frequently been told of some old man, then dead, from whom I could have got certain songs had I been a few months earlier in my inquiries. Although from some country singers I have met with the utmost sympathy and aid, yet from others, from shyness or from a difficulty of seeing the utility of collecting these old things, I have not found my task a light one.

Another source of trouble has been the notation of tunes from singers who, by reason of great age and quavering voices, sang the melody flat and out of tune.

The type of tunes, here gathered together, is one which never got into print, for they were sung by a different class of people to those catered for by the music publisher.

Of course the tunes in the present collection vary very much as to age, but the older class of airs is, I think I may safely say, the remnants or survival of early minstrel melody. Such (and I believe musical antiquaries will bear me out), are—"The Three Ravens," "The Knight and Shepherd's Daughter," "The Dowie Dens of Yarrow," "Lord Thomas and Fair Eleanor," and several more. Of a later period, but still, I feel sure, very early specimens of melody, are—"My True Love once he courted me," "Green Bushes," "The Pretty Ploughboy," "The Nightingale," "The Sprig of Thyme," "Polly Oliver's Ramble," etc. While airs of the last century appear to find examples in—"Colin and Phœbe," "The Indian Lass," "The Spotted Cow," "Young Bucks a-hunting go," "The White Hare," besides many others.

The earlier airs breathe a peculiar plaintive strain such as can be fully imagined would be the tone of the singer of that day. This would be the woman of the house who sat spinning, while her husband or sweetheart was away swashbucklering, either as a lord or a vassal, and most likely to be brought home dead, dying, or maimed.

The incidents of the story to which such airs were joined were always more or less of a melancholy character; the tune in the minor mode, of one strain, simple in structure, of little compass, and being queer and odd in interval. As time got on, the airs lost a good deal of their ruggedness, and towards the middle of the last century became more ornamental in character; still, these traditional tunes were never of the scholarly type of the published melodies; but that they have no lack of beautiful melody it is needless to say. From the early days these songs have passed down from mouth to mouth, and as printed music and musical instruments became more common, they were abandoned for newer and more fashionable music, till it was left for the cottage to preserve what the hall had cast aside.

Many of the airs somewhat later have been evolved by rustic fiddlers or crowders for the amusement of a rustic audience, and, like their predecessors, passed down in a country side for many ages. They would be carried from place to place by pedlars and by journeymen who travelled to ply their trade.

The question naturally arises, what changes have the tunes undergone in their passage down to our own time? Undoubtedly, in many instances, much corruption has crept in : in some cases by the wilful alterations of singers and performers, and in other instances by reason of imperfect acquirement of the air. Never having been fixed by any printed or written standard, each singer has unconsciously omitted, added to, or changed the strain, more or less according to his musical ear or the retentiveness of his memory. This being the case, it is much to be wondered at that some few tunes are found so little altered in different districts, and it satisfactorily accounts for the variations in others. The fact certainly remains that tradition is wonderfully accurate, and this is so in more things than in old tunes.

Many instances could be given which would satisfactorily prove this, and show the tenacity with which certain tunes have held together while transmitted orally.

In the course of my search for materials for the present work, I have found this in many instances to be satisfactorily proved. I have had many old airs sung to me which I have been told had descended down, strictly orally, from some far back relative, the period of time covered being from fifty to a hundred years. In the instances I name I have been able to verify the airs from printed copies contemporary with the original singers, and, in most cases, I have found a wonderful accuracy. In these examples, none of the singers had sufficient musical knowledge to read or play from the "prick."

In the present collection some tunes may be quoted to bear out this statement. The first version of "The Banks of Sweet Dundee" is sung, to my own knowledge, as near note for note as possible in places so widely apart as the South of Scotland, and the North and West Ridings of Yorkshire, and in Berkshire and Oxfordshire. There are also other tunes to which this song is sung in certain districts, but this particular setting I have myself heard in the places named. None of the singers of the song can have ever had any written or printed copy of the air to aid their memory, for, I believe I am perfectly warranted in saying that this set of the tune is here in print for the first time.

"The Summer Morning" may also be mentioned as an air which has a like traditional existence in different parts of England. The trifling variations of "Forty Miles"* is also worth noticing. In general, where an original melody has some degree of intricacy, it is found either greatly changed in different districts or a totally fresh air used for the song. "Polly Oliver," "Henry Martin," "My True Love once he courted me," and others in the volume now before the reader are examples of this. In such instances the change is due to a singer who, unable to thoroughly master the air, either boldly invents a new one or uses for the song one with which he is more familiar. In later times, when reading became a little more general in country districts, the ballad sheets would give a certain stability to the words, which the music had not the advantage of, for had the air been also printed with the ballad (a thing which scarcely ever occurred), the rustic who bought the sheet would have been no wiser. There are even now in country places old fiddlers who, while being good performers of this class of old airs and of country dances, openly boast that they never knew a

---

* It may be worth while reminding the reader that the distance, "Forty Miles," is no fanciful or haphazard statement. In the days of journeymen who travelled with their kit of tools on their shoulders from town to town to seek work, forty miles per day was the regulation distance, and the picture the song gives of a tired and wet traveller seeking admittance at a farm cottage is a natural one.

written note of music in their lives, and maintain that they who are ignorant in this particular matter are the better performers.

This circumstance, besides the additional one of the typographical difficulties in way of music printing, has kept the ballad printer (generally a very poor and ignorant man) to the words alone. The corruptions that have crept in by reason of the blunders of the reciter or the illiterateness of the printer have frequently turned a ballad, originally good, into an absurdity ; it must also be conceded that the rustic muse produced better melody than poetry or even rhyme.

The reader of these old songs and ballads must not criticise them from a modern standpoint ; they have their place in our literature, and pleased the simple audience to which they were originally addressed.

FRANK KIDSON.

Traditional Tunes.

THE THREE RAVENS.

THE air here following bears to my mind every appearance of antiquity. It is a different strain to the now well-known tune to the same song which William Chappell prints in *Popular Music of the Olden Time*, taken from *Melismata*, 1611, and which had been previously unearthed by Sibbald in the new series of *The Vocal Magazine*, Edinburgh, *circa* 1800.

I am favoured with the copy here presented by Mr. John Holmes, of Roundhay, who first heard it about 1825 from his mother's singing. This was in a remote village among the Derbyshire hills, most aptly named Stoney Middleton.

Although the air is not the same with the better known copy, the words differ but slightly from the original. Mr. Holmes tells me that he heard a Danish gentleman play this same tune, so familiar to him, on the violin, and was informed by him that it had been current among the people in Denmark.

THE THREE RAVENS.

There were three ra-vens on a tree, A-down, a-down, a der ry down,There

were three ra-vens on a tree. Heigh ho ! The middlemost ra-ven said to me, 'There

lies a dead man at yon tree. A-down, a-down, a der-ry down, Heigh ho !

There were three ravens on a tree,
    A-down, a-down, a derry down,
There were three ravens on a tree,
    Heigh ho !
The middlemost raven said to me,
" There lies a dead man at yon tree,"
    A-down, a-down, a derry down,
    Heigh ho !

There comes his lady full of woe,
    A-down, a-down, a derry down,
There comes his lady full of woe,
    Heigh ho !
There comes his lady full of woe,
  . . . . . as she could go,
    A-down, a-down, a derry down,
    Heigh ho !

" Who's this that's killed my own true love,
    A-down, a-down, a derry down,
Who's this that's killed my own true love,
    Heigh ho !
I hope in heaven he'll never rest,
Nor e'er enjoy that blessed place."
    A-down, a-down, a derry down,
    Heigh ho !

Though by no means complete, the above is given as a traditional fragment for the purpose of comparison. The ballad has been known in Scotland under the title, "The Twa Corbies." See Scott's *Minstrelsy of the Scottish Borders*, Motherwell's *Minstrelsy*, 1827, and other ballad collections. Motherwell prints a traditional air for the "Three Ravens," as sung in Scotland, but it is unlike either the one here set forth or the one in *Melismata*.

CHEVY CHACE.

THE following setting of the ballad used to be sung in a doleful voice by ballad singers in the West Riding of Yorkshire. It is not the same with the many published airs to which Chevy Chace is found united. Mr. Wm. Cheetham, of Horsforth, supplies the present version.

The ballad itself is much too long and too well known for insertion here.

CHEVY CHACE.

God pros-per long our noble king, Our lives, and safe-ties all ; A

no-ble hunt - ing did there once In Chev-y Chace be - fall !

God prosper long our noble king,
Our lives and safeties all ;
A woeful hunting did there once
In Chevy Chace befall.

To drive the deer with hound and horn,
Earl Percy took his way :
The child may rue that is unborn
The hunting of that day.
Etc. etc..

———◆———

THE KNIGHT AND SHEPHERD'S DAUGHTER.

THIS is an example of a very ancient ballad, which has come down traditionally to our own time. The tune, from its peculiar structure, is, I am confident, quite contemporary with very early copies of the words. It used to be sung many years ago by the Leeds mill girls, and was one of the "fly boat songs," as they were named. This title was given on account of the lads and lasses who invested their pence in fly boat rides at fairs, etc., singing such like ditties. The chief characteristic of a "fly boat song," was its easy swing and vigour.

My friend, Mr. Benjamin Holgate, of Leeds, to whom I am in-debted for so many excellent airs in this collection, supplies the air and fragment of song.

Like the generality of old ballads, the words are found under many guises, both in English and in Scottish ballad books.

It seems to have been first printed by Bishop Percy in the *Reliques*, who informs us that it is taken from an old black letter copy, and is mentioned by Hearne as being popular in Queen Elizabeth's time. There is also a quotation from the ballad in Fletcher's plays, "The Knight of the Burning Pestle," and in the "Pilgrim." A black letter copy is preserved among the Roxburghe collection of broadsides.

The Scottish versions are variously titled: "Earl Richard," in Motherwell's *Minstrelsy*, 1827, "Earl Richard, the Queen's Brother," in Buchan's *Ancient Ballads of the North*, 1828, and there is also a long copy of "Earl Richard" in Kinloch's ballads.

Scott quotes a verse in the "Abbot"—

> "Oh, some do call me Jack, sweet love,
> And some do call me Gill;
> But when I ride to Holyrood,
> They call me Wilful Will."

The fragment obtained in Leeds, and here in part presented, differs somewhat from the other versions of the ballad, but only enough can be given to serve as a vehicle for the beautiful and simple air.

THE KNIGHT, AND SHEPHERD'S DAUGHTER.

There was a shep-herd's daugh-ter, Who sat up-on yon hill, There came a young man rid-ing by, Who swore he'd have his will. Fol lol lay, Fol lol di did-dle lol di day.

There was a shepherd's daughter,
Who kept sheep on yon hill ;
There came a young man riding by,
Who swore he'd have his will.
Fol lol lay, &c.

He took her by the lilly white hand,
And by her silken sleeve ;
. . . .
Fol lol lay, &c.

. . . .
Or tell to me your name.
Fol lol lay, &c.

"Oh, some they call me Jack, sweetheart,
And some they call me Will ;
But when I ride the king's high-gate,
But name is sweet William."
Fol lol lay, &c.

The use of the term, "King's high-gate" for the king's high-road, is noticeable as having a distinct Yorkshire ring with it.

Chappell gives an air to the above, taken from Playford's *Dancing Master*, called the "Shepherd's Daughter," and Motherwell inserts a tune for "Earl Richard." They both have, of course, nothing in common with the Leeds version.

THE DOWIE DENS OF YARROW.

I OBTAINED this traditional version of the ballad, as well as the fine old tune, from Mrs. Calvert, of Gilnockie, in Eskdale, where, and in Liddesdale, it is occasionally heard. Mrs. Calvert originally obtained it on the braes of Yarrow from her grandmother, who was the celebrated Tibbie Shiel, the humble friend of Sir Walter Scott and James Hogg.

Sir Walter Scott was the first to publish the ballad in his *Minstrelsy of the Scottish Borders*, where he states that it was a great favourite among the inhabitants of Ettrick forest. Scott's version differs much from the one now printed, and an air which is fitted to it in the 1833 edition of Scott's poems, Vol. III., bears no resemblance to Mrs. Calvert's air.

The Minstrelsy version commences—

> " Late at e'en, drinking the wine,
>   And ere they paid the lawing,
> They set a combat them between,
>   To fight it in the dawing."

Several other copies are found in the Scottish collections. Mother-well has one from the recitation of an old woman in the west of Scotland. Buchan in his *Ancient Ballads of the North* has another which more nearly resembles the one I now print; and Aytoun, in *Ballads of Scotland*, 1858, gives an excellent version, along with some very pertinent remarks respecting the ballad as printed by Scott.

THE DOWIE DENS OF YARROW.

There liv'd a la - dy in the west, I ne'er could find her mar - row:
She was courted by nine gen-tle-men, And a ploughboy lad in Yar-row.

> There lived a lady in the west—
>   I ne'er could find her marrow;
> She was courted by nine gentlemen,
>   And a ploughboy lad in Yarrow.
>
> These nine sat drinking at the wine,
>   Sat drinking wine in Yarrow;
> They made a vow among themselves,
>   To fight for her in Yarrow.
>
> She washed his face, she kaimed his hair,
>   As oft she'd done before, O !
> She made him like a knight sae bright,
>   To fight for her in Yarrow.

As he walked up yon high, high hill,
  And down by the holmes of Yarrow ;
There he saw nine armèd men,
  Come to fight with him in Yarrow.

" There's nine of you, there's one of me,
  It's an unequal marrow ;
But I'll fight you all one by one,
  On the dowie dens of Yarrow."

There he slew, and there they flew,
  And there he wounded sorely ;
Till her brother, John, he came in beyond,
  And pierced his heart most foully.

" Go home, go home, thou false young man,
  And tell thy sister, Sarah,
That her true love, John, lies dead and gone,
  On the dowie dens of Yarrow."

" Oh, father, dear, I dreamed a dream,
  I'm afraid it will bring sorrow ;
I dreamed I was pulling the heather bell,
  In the dowie dens of Yarrow."

" Oh, daughter, dear, I read your dream,
  I doubt it will prove sorrow ;
For your true love, John, lies dead and gone,
  On the dowie dens of Yarrow."

As she walked up yon high, high hill,
  And down by the holmes of Yarrow,
There she saw her true love, John,
  Lying pale and dead on Yarrow.

Her hair it being three quarters long,
  The colour it was yellow ;
She wrapped it round his middle sma',
  And carried him hame to Yarrow.

" Oh. father, dear, you've seven sons,
  You may wed them a' to-morrow ;
But a fairer flower I never saw,
  Than the lad I loved in Yarrow."

This fair maid being great with child,
  It filled her heart with sorrow ;
She died within her lover's arms,
  Between that day and morrow.

Sir Walter Scott gives an account of the supposed circumstances of this story, but other accounts are also to be found which point to different actors. What the real facts of the case were can never now be known, but it cannot be doubted but that the ballad is founded on some tragic deed which has really happened.

In the early and lawless period in which the original ballad was produced, no hesitation would be felt in removing, either by treachery or in fair fight, a suitor of lower birth who had dared to aspire to a daughter of a family of position. The "Dowie Dens of Yarrow" appears to chronicle some such event.

GEORDIE.

THE air now given resembles in a marked degree the traditional tune, the "Dowie Dens of Yarrow" just previously printed.

It was obtained for me by Mr. Charles Lolley, of Leeds, from the district of Howden, in Yorkshire. A fragment of a version of the Scotch ballad, "Geordie," was fitted to it, but one which appears to have formed part of a version of the piece not to be found in print.

> " My Geordie he shall hang in chains,
> In chains of gold and silver,
> For stealing of the king's white deer."

. . . .

One of the original issues of the ballad appears in black letter in the Roxburghe collection of broadsides. It is entitled, " *A Lamentable New Ditty made upon the Death of a worthy gentleman, George Stoole, dwelling sometime on Gateside Moor and sometime at Newcastle, in Northumberland, with his penitent end, to a delicate Scottish Tune.*"

George Stoole was executed in 1610.

James Hogg prints the ballad in his *Jacobite Relics*, and in Johnson's *Scot's Musical Museum*, Vol. IV., 1792, there is one totally different, a few verses of which are here given, to fit the traditional tune which Mr. Lolley favours me with.

GEORDIE.

There was a bat-tle in the North, And no-bles there were ma - ny, And
they hae killed Sir Char - lie Hay, And laid the wyte on Geor - die.

There was a battle in the North,
   And nobles there were many ;
And they hae killed Sir Charlie Hay,
   And laid the wyte on Geordie.

O, he has written a lang letter,
   He sent it to his lady—
"Ye maun come up to Edinbro' town,
   To see what words o' Geordie."

When first she looked the letter on,
   She was baith red and rosy ;
But she hadna read a word but twa,
   Till she wallow't like a lily.

     . . . .

And she has mounted her gude grey steed,
   Her menzie a' gaed wi' her ;
And she did neither eat nor drink,
   Till Edinbro' town did see her.

At first, appear'd the fatal block,
   And syne the axe to head him,
And Geordie coming down the stair,
   Wi' bands of iron on him.

     . . . .

O, she's down on her bended knees—
   I wat she's pale and weary—
"O ! pardon, pardon, noble king,
   And gie me back my dearie.

" I hae borne seven sons to my Geordie, dear,
      The seventh ne'er saw his daddy ;
O ! pardon, pardon, noble king,
      Pity a waefu' lady."

" Gar bid the headin' man mak haste,"
      Our king replied fu lordly ;
" O ! noble king, tak a' that's mine,
      But gie me back my Geordie."

            .   .   .   .

An aged lord at the king's right hand,
      Says, " Noble king, but hear me,
" Gar her tell down five thousand pounds,
      And gie her back her dearie."

Some gae her marks, some gae her crowns,
      Some gae her dollars many ;
And she's tell'd down five thousand pounds,
      And gotten again her dearie.

He claspit her by the middle sma',
      And he kissed her lips sae rosy—
" The fairest flower o' woman kind,
      Is my sweet, bonnie lady !"

Stenhouse, in his notes to Johnson's *Museum*, says that Robert
Burns obtained this ballad for Johnson, and that it relates to George,
Earl of Huntly, who was sent by the Queen Regent of Scotland to
Shetland, in 1554, to seize a certain person, which he failed to do.
He was imprisoned and his estates forfeited, but afterwards came
again into favour.

———◆●◆———

THE OUTLANDISH KNIGHT.

A SINGULAR ballad of the Bluebeard type which formerly
      had a wide spread popularity in England and Scotland. The
same thing is found in the folk lore of Sweden and Germany. The
first Scottish version published was in David Herd's collection,
1776, as " May Colvin," and afterwards other copies appear in later
gatherings, as " May Collean " and " False Sir John." Tradition,

it is said, points out the real actors in the drama, and gives names to the places wherein it was enacted; but, as these vary in each district where the ballad is or was recited, no reliance can be placed upon it. For particulars see Chamber's *Ballads*, 1829, and Child's collection, 1857.

The "Outlandish Knight" is the English copy of the story, and it was first edited in a volume issued by the Percy Society, by Mr. J. H. Dixon; *Scottish Traditional Versions of Ancient Ballads*, 1846. I am in possession of a copy of it on a broadside in a similar form, but named "The Old Beau."

All copies, both Scottish and English, preserve the parrot incident.

The air was obtained in the North Riding of Yorkshire, and is certainly an early tune. Another air to the same words may be found in *Northumbrian Minstrelsy*, and others, differing from each other, to which the "May Colvin" version of it were sung, are in R. A. Smith's *Scottish Minstrel*, Vol. III., *circa* 1821, Motherwell's *Minstrely*, 1827, and Christie's *Traditional Airs*, Vol. II.

THE OUTLANDISH KNIGHT.

An Out-landish knight from the Northlands came, And he came a woo-ing to me; He promised he'd take me to the Northlands, And there he'd mar-ry me.

An Outlandish knight from the North lands came,
    And he came a wooing to me ;
He promised he'd take me to the North lands,
    And there he'd marry me.

" Come fetch me some of your father's gold,
    And some of your mother's fee,
And two of the best nags out of the stable,
    Where they stand thirty and three.'

She fetched him some of her father's gold,
    And some of her mother's fee,
And two of the best nags out of the stable,
    Where they stood thirty and three.

She mounted on her milk-white steed,
    He on the dapple grey ;
They rode till they came unto the sea-side,
    Three hours before it was day.

" Light off, light off, thy milk-white steed,
    And deliver it unto me ;
Six pretty maids have I drowned here,
    And thou the seventh shalt be.

" Pull off, pull off thy silken gown,
    And deliver it unto me ;
Methinks it looks too rich and gay,
    To rot in the salt sea.

" Pull off, pull off thy silken stays,
    And deliver them unto me ;
Methinks they are too fine and gay,
    To rot in the salt sea.

" Pull off, pull off thy Holland smock,
    And deliver it unto me ;
Methinks it looks too rich and gay,
    To rot in the salt sea."

" If I must pull off my Holland smock,
    Pray, turn thy back on me ;
For it is not fitting that such a ruffian
    A naked woman should see."

He turned his back towards her,
    And viewed the leaves so green ;
She catched him round the middle so small,
    And tumbled him into the stream.

He dropped high, and he dropped low,
    Until he came to the side ;—
" Catch hold of my hand, my pretty maiden,
    And I will make you my bride."

" Lie there, lie there, thou false-hearted man,
    Lie there instead of me ;
Six pretty maids hast thou drowned here,
    And the seventh has drowned thee."

She mounted on her milk-white steed,
    And led the dapple grey ;
She rode till she came to her own father's hall,
    Three hours before it was day.

The parrot being in the window so high,
    Hearing the lady, did say—
" I'm afraid that some ruffian has led you astray,
    That you have tarried so long away."

" Don't prittle nor prattle, my pretty parrot,
    Nor tell any tales of me ;
And thy cage shall be made of glittering gold,
    Although it is made of the tree !"

The king being in the chamber so high,
    And hearing the parrot, did say—
" What ails you, what ails you, my pretty parrot,
    That you prattle so long before day ?"

" It's no laughing matter," the parrot did say,
    " That so loudly I call unto thee ;
For the cats have got into the window so high,
    And I'm afraid they will have me."

" Well turned, well turned, my pretty parrot,
    Well turned, well turned for me ;
Thy cage shall be made of the glittering gold,
    And the door of the best ivory."

HENRY MARTIN.

FOR this very singular old fragment I am in the first instance
    indebted to Mr. Wm. Cheetham, of Horsforth, who has
remembered a portion of the words and the tune from his boyhood.
In his letter enclosing the fragment, Mr. Cheetham says—" As to
the fragments of Henry Martin, it is something to have got even the
name of the old ditty. To the best of my recollection, it ended by
Master Henry being hanged—' to maintain his two brothers and
he'—and very properly, though sad. It must relate to the
buccaneering times, about a hundred and fifty or two hundred
years ago. It was sung by a *very* old woman—a bobbin winder—

in my mother's youth, about ninety years ago, and my recollection
of the air is from hearing it sixty years ago. I only wish we had
the words as accurate as the air."

Mr. Cheetham's version is as follows—

HENRY MARTIN.

(First Version.)

There lived three brothers in merry Scotland,
In merry Scotland lived three brothers ;
And they did cast lots which should rob on the sea,
To maintain his two brothers and he.

And the lot it did light on Henry Martin—
The youngest of all the brothers three—
And he went a roaming on the salt sea,
To maintain his two brothers and he.

And when they had sailèd five days and more,
On a rich merchant ship coming down they then bore,
As he went a roaming on the salt sea,
To maintain his two brothers and he.

The rich merchant ship got wounded by he,
And right down to the bottom of the salt sea went she,
As he went a roaming on the salt sea,
To maintain his two brothers and he.

I think that there can be no doubt but that this is a portion of an early Scottish ballad, dating from a period before the time Mr. Cheetham supposes. I can find nothing in print among the Scottish or English ballads having the same story, and I have failed to find the ballad on a broadside.

Upon inquiry I found that among the fisher folk at Flamborough in Yorkshire, the ballad was known, and with a little difficulty, by the judicious expenditure of tobacco, I was enabled to note down the following:—

HENRY MARTIN.

(Second Version.)

In Scotland there liv'd three brothers; of late, In Scotland there liv'd brothers three, And they did cast lots which should rob on the sea To maintain his two bro-thers and he.

In Scotland there lived three brothers of late,
   In Scotland there lived brothers three ;
Now, the youngest cast lots with the other two,
   Which should go rob on the salt sea.

The lot it did fall to bold Henry Martin—
   The youngest of all the three ;
And he had to turn robber all on the salt seas,
   To maintain his two brothers and he.

He had not been sailing past a long winter's night,
   Past a long winter's night before day,
Before he espied a lofty, fine ship,
   Come sailing all on the salt sea.

"O ! where are you bound for ?" cried Henry Martin,
   "O ! where are you bound for ?" cried he ;
" I'm a rich loaded ship bound for fair England,
   I pray you to let me pass free."

"O, no! O, no!" cried Henry Martin,
  "O, no! that never can be;
Since I have turned robber all on the salt sea,
  To maintain my two brothers and me.

"Heave down your main tack, likewise your main tie,
  And lig yourself under my lee;
For your rich glowing gold I will take it away,
  And your fair bodies drown in the salt sea."

Then broadside to broadside they merrily fought,
  For fully two hours or three,
When, by chance, Henry Martin, gave her a broadside,
  And right down to the bottom went she.

Bad news! bad news! unto old England,
  Bad news I tell unto thee;
For your rich glowing gold is all wasted away,
  And your mariners are drown'd in the salt sea.

As will be perceived, the air is totally different, and probably nothing like so old as the first version. The song is, howeve, more complete. In both copies the words have been no doubt much corrupted in their passage down to our own time.

** Since the above was at press, I find that the Rev. S. Baring-Gould has published a version of Henry Martin in his "Songs of the West," with an air different to either of the foregoing.

LORD BATEMAN.

MANY are the airs which have been set to the popular street ballad, "Lord Bateman." Mrs. Holt, of Alderhill, Meanwood, supplies the following, varying from any of the sets which I have hitherto seen of the tune.

The common version of the words is undoubtedly much corrupted from a very early metrical poem, and there are numberless copies printed in the English and Scottish ballad books, which were formerly current in a traditional form throughout the land. They are all in general much longer than the one now popular, hereunder given. The story in all these is of a Christian knight, who sailing into an eastern land is imprisoned, and afterwards released by the daughter of his captor. She afterwards follows him across the seas and arrives at the opportune moment, when the knight, forgetting her who befriended him, is about to wed another lady.

It has been asserted, with every appearance of truth, that the hero of the tale was Gilbert àBecket, father of Saint Thomas àBecket of Canterbury, who in the early times of the Crusades was captured as in the ballad, released, and followed to London by the lady.

She is said to have known no more than two words of English: "Gilbert" and "London," and to have cried the first through London streets until she found her lover. Fanciful as the legend appears, it is supported by the fact that every ballad known on the subject gives the name of the knight as a greater or lesser corruption of Becket. For instance: "Young Bekie," "Lord Beichan," "Lord Bateman," etc.

For the various copies of the ballad in its Scottish form, see Jamieson's *Popular Ballads*, Kinloch's *Scottish Ballads*, Mother-well's and Buchan's collections, etc.; a lengthy English version is found in Dixon's *Ancient Poems, Ballads, and Songs*, printed for the Percy Society.

The broadside version from Catnach's press is the one remembered by Mrs. Holt, and here given.

The various tunes to "Lord Bateman," all different to the following, are to be found in *The Loving Ballad of Lord Bateman* (said to be edited by Dickens), illustrated by George Cruikshank; *Northumbrian Minstrelsy*, Christie's *Traditional Airs*, and *Sussex Songs*.

LORD BATEMAN.

Lord Bateman was a no-ble lord, A no-ble lord of high de-gree; He put him-self all on a ship, Some foreign coun-tries he would go see.

Lord Bateman was a noble Lord,
  A noble Lord of high degree ;
He put himself all on a ship,
  Some foreign countries he would go see.

He sailèd east and sailèd west,
  Until he came to fair Turkey,
Where he was taken and put in prison,
  Until his life was quite weary.

And in this prison there grew a tree,
  It grew so stout and it grew so strong,
Where he was chained by the middle,
  Until his life was almost gone.

The Turk he had an only daughter,
  The fairest creature ever my eyes did see ;
She stole the keys of her father's prison,
  And swore Lord Bateman she would set free !

" Have you got houses, have you got lands?
  Or does Northumberland belong to thee?
What would you give to the fair young lady,
  That out of prison would set you free ?"

" I have got houses, I have got lands,
  And half Northumberland belongs to me ;
I'll give it all to the fair young lady,
  That out of prison would set me free."

Oh, then she took him to her father's palace,
  And gave to him the best of wine,
And every health she drank unto him—
  " I wish, Lord Bateman, that you were mine."

" Now, for seven long years, I'll make a vow,
  For seven long years, and keep it strong,
If you will wed no other woman,   ·
  That I will wed no other man."

Oh, then she took him to her father's harbour,
  And gave to him a ship of fame ;
" Farewell, farewell, my dear Lord Bateman,
  I'm afraid I shall never see you again."

Now, seven long years were gone and past,
  And fourteen long days well known to me
She packed up her gay clothing,
  And Lord Bateman she would go see.

And then she came to Lord Bateman's castle,
So boldly now she rang the bell ;
" Who's there ?" cried the young porter,
" Who's there—now come unto me tell ?"

" Oh, is this Lord Bateman's castle,
And is his Lordship here within ;"
" O yes, O yes," cried the proud young porter,
He's just taking his young bride in."

" Oh, then tell him to send me a slice of bread,
And a bottle of the best wine ;
And not forgetting the fair young lady,
That did release him when close confined."

Away, away, went that proud young porter,
Away, away, and away went he,
Until he came to Lord Bateman's door,
Down on his bended knees fell he.

" What news, what news, my young porter,
What news have you brought unto me ?"
" There is the fairest of all young ladies,
That ever my two eyes did see.

" She has got rings on every finger,
And round one of them she has got three ;
And such gay gold hanging round her middle,
That would buy Northumberland for thee.

" She tells you to send her a slice of bread,
And a bottle of the best wine ;
And not forgetting the fair young lady,
That did release you when close confined."

Lord Bateman then in a passion flew,
And broke his sword in splinters three,
Saying, " I will give all my father's riches,
If that Sophia has crossed the sea."

Then up spoke this bride's young mother,
Who never was heard to speak so free—
" You'll not forget my only daughter,
If Sophia has crossed the sea."

" I own I made a bride of your daughter,
She's neither the better nor worse for me ;
She came to me with a horse and saddle,
She may go home in a coach and three."

Lord Bateman prepared another marriage,
With both their hearts so full 'of glee ;
" I'll range no more in foreign countries,
Now since Sophia has cross'd the sea. "

———◆———

BARBARA ALLEN.

FEW ballads have had a more lasting popularity than "Cruel Barbara Allen." The story is common both in England and Scotland, and it may, I have no doubt, be equally well known in Ireland. It is quite needless to say that by the very reason of its being such a favourite there are endless versions of both the song and the tune. The original composition must date from a very early period, but the traditional versions now extant are in general so corrupted as to make a very doleful and pitiable story into that which might provoke more laughter than sympathy.

Early forms of it are found on black letter broadsides, and a mention is made by Pepys in his diary under January 2nd, 1665-6. Speaking of Mrs. Knipp, he says :—" with whom I. sang, and in perfect pleasure it was to hear her sing, and especially her little Scotch song of Barbary Allen." Both Scotch and English versions of the ballad are in Percy's Reliques, and the Scotch one in Allan Ramsay's *Tea Table Miscellany*, 1724.

There are two different tunes to Barbara Allen commonly printed, the one best known first appearing in Chappell's *National English Airs*, 1838, and the other being found in Scottish song collections. The earliest copy of this I have seen is in Oswald's *Caledonian Pocket Companion*, Book II., *circa* 1750, and after this period, in a small collection of Macgibbon's. It is also in Johnson's *Musical Museum*, and in later works.

The three tunes, however, here given are, I believe, now for the first time printed, although they have been current in different parts of the country for many years. They are quite distinct from any of the airs quoted above.

The first here following, noted down from Mr. Holgate, is from the singing of an English girl in Ghent, some forty years ago, and this version, with a different termination, is heard in the West Riding of Yorkshire.

It is so well known and so easily accessible that is is perhaps not worth while to reproduce the entire words, which are for this setting as in Percy.

BARBARA ALLEN.

In Reading town, where I was born,There was a fair maid dwelling, Made

e... y youth cry," Well-a-day!" Her name was Bar-ba-ra Al-len.

(Another termination.)

weil a day! Her name was Bar - bara Al - len.

In Reading town, where I was born,
There was a fair maid dwelling,
Made every youth cry, "Well-a-day !"—
Her name was Barbara Allen.
Etc. etc.

The second version is from the Northallerton district, and varies from the usual words. I take the air of this to be of an early date, and when sweetly sung is excellent.

BARBARA ALLEN.

(Second Version.)

In Scotland I was born and bred, Oh! there it was my dwel-ling; I
court-ed there a pret-ty maid, Oh, her name was Bar bara Al - len.

In Scotland I was born and bred,
O, there it was my dwelling ;
I courted there a pretty maid,
O, her name was Barbara Allen.

I courted her in summer time,
I courted her in winter ;
For six long years I courted her,
A-thinking I should win her.

. . . .

The third version of Barbara Allen is, like the preceding, also from the North Riding of Yorkshire, from the singing of Mr. A. Wardill, Goathland.

It has a resemblance to the second set, but lacks in sweetness what the other possesses. I also got the same tune to a similar copy of the ballad at Bradford.

BARBARA ALLEN.

(Third Version.)

In Reading town there I was born, In Scot-land was my dwel - ling; Oh!
there I court-ed a pret-ty fair maid, Her name was Barbara Al - len; Oh!
there I court-ed a pret-ty fair maid, Her name was Bar-bara Al - len.

In Reading town, there I was born,
  In Scotland was my dwelling ;
O, there I courted a pretty, fair maid—
  Her name was Barbara Allen.
      O, there I courted, etc.

I courted her for months and years,
  Thinking that I should gain her ;
And I oft times vowed and did declare
  No other man should have her.

I sent a man to yonder town,
  To ask for Barbara Allen,
Saying, "You must come to my master's house,
  If your name be Barbara Allen."

So slowly she put on her clothes,
  So slowly she came to him ;
And when she got to his bedside,
  "Young man," she said, "you're dying."

      . . . .

If you look under my pillow,
  You'll find a napkin lying,
And it is soaked with my heart's blood,
  For the love of Barbara Allen.

He put his hand right out of bed,
  Thinking to draw her nigh him ;
But she whipped her heels and away she ran,
  Straightway from him she flew.

So he turned his face unto the wall,
  And death came slowly to him ;
"Adieu, adieu to all my friends,
  Farewell to Barbara Allen."

As she was walking across yon fields,
  She heard his death-bell tolling,
And every toll it seemed to say—
  Hard-hearted Barbara Allen.

      . . . .

" O, dear mother, make me my bed,
  And make it fit to die on ;
There's a young man died for me to-day,
  And I'll die for him to-morrow."

      . . . .

> And he did die on one good day,
> And she died on the morrow ;
> O, he did die for the love of her,
> And she did die for sorrow.

A comparison with Percy's copy will show how much the above has suffered by being handed down traditionally.

LORD THOMAS AND FAIR ELEANOR.

THE air is different to the printed set, which is first found in Sandy's *Christmas Carols*, 1833, or to the Scottish air, "Lord Thomas and Fair Annet."

The present copy is from the Whitby district, forwarded by a relative of the editor. The words are some of the verses from a rare and old broadside, entitled, *A Tragical Ballad of the Unfortunate Loves of Lord Thomas and Fair Eleanor, circa* 1740. It is the same with a copy which appeared in *Old Ballads*, 1723. The ballad is an early one, Ritson speaking of it as "having every appearance of a minstrel song." It is found under a Scotch dress in "Lord Thomas and Fair Annet," the story being essentially the same.

LORD THOMAS AND FAIR ELEANOR.

Lord Thom - as was a bold fo - rest - er, And a
cha - ser of the king's deer; Fair E - lea - nor was a
fine wo - man, And Lord Thom-as he lov - ed her dear.

Lord Thomas he was a bold forester,
　And a chaser of the king's deer ;
Fair Eleanor was a fine woman,
　And Lord Thomas loved her dear.

" Come, riddle my riddle, dear mother," he said,
　" And riddle us both in one ;
Whether I shall marry with sweet Eleanor,
　And let the brown girl alone ?"

"The brown girl she has got houses and land,
　Fair Eleanor she has got none ;
Therefore, I charge thee on my blessing,
　Bring me the brown girl home."

And as it befel on a holiday,
　As many more do beside,
Lord Thomas went to fair Eleanor,
　That should have been his bride.

　　　. . . . . . .

" What news, what news, Lord Thomas ?" she said,
　" What news hast thou brought to me ?"
" I am come to bid thee to my wedding,
　And that's sad news for thee."

" O, God forbid ! Lord Thomas," she said,
　That such a thing should ever be done ;
I thought to have been thy bride myself,
　And thou been the bridegroom."

　　　. . . . .

She clothed herself in gallant attire,
　And her merry men in green ;
And as she rode through every place,
　They took her to be some queen.

When she came to Lord Thomas's gate,
　She knocked at the ring ;
And who was so ready as Lord Thomas,
　To let fair Eleanor in.

　　　. . . . .

" Is this your bride ?" fair Eleanor said,
　" Methinks she looks wondrous brown ;
Thou might'st have had as fair a woman,
　As ever trod upon the ground."

" Despise her not," Lord Thomas he said,
  Despise her not unto me ;
For better I love thy little finger,
  Than all her whole body."

This brown girl had a little penknife,
  Which was both keen and sharp,
And betwixt the short ribs and the long,
  She prick'd fair Eleanor to the heart.

" O Christ, now save me," Lord Thomas he said,
  " Methinks thou looks wondrous wan ;
Thou us'd to look as good a colour,
  As ever the sun shone on."

" O, art thou blind, Lord Thomas ?" she said,
  " Or canst thou not very well see ;
O, dost thou not see my own heart's blood,
  Runs trickling down my knee."

    . . . .

Lord Thomas he had a sword by his side,
  As he walked about the hall ;
He cut his bride's head from her shoulders,
  And flung it against the wall.

He set his sword upon the ground,
  And the point against his heart ;
There never was three lovers, sure,
  That sooner did depart.

——◆——

SCARBOROUGH FAIR.

PARADOXES and riddles frequently have formed the subject
of fireside stories and song. "Scarborough Fair" is one of
the latter. The original of it is an old ballad (to be found also in
Scandinavian folk-song), called "The Elfin Knight." The English
versions of this is found on black letter broadsides, and is reprinted
in most of the ballad collections. In various parts of the country
"Scarborough" Fair becomes "Whittingham" Fair, or any other
town the reciter chooses to name that is best known to him. In
Cromek's "Remains of Nithsdale and Galloway Song," 1810,

Allan Cunningham has woven up the song into a lengthy piece called "The Bridegroom Darg."

The present copy, including the tune, used to be sung by a ballad singer in Whitby streets twenty or thirty years ago, and is still remembered in the district.

SCARBOROUGH FAIR.

Oh! where are you going? To Scar - bro' fair,
Sa - vour - y sage rose - ma - ry and thyme: Re - mem - ber
me to a lass that lives there, For once she was a true love of mine.

"O, where are you going?" "To Scarborough fair,"
Savoury sage, rosemary, and thyme ;
"Remember me to a lass who lives there,
For once she was a true love of mine.

"And tell her to make me a cambric shirt,
Savoury sage, rosemary, and thyme,
Without any seam or needlework,
And then she shall be a true love of mine.

"And tell her to wash it in yonder dry well,
Savoury sage, rosemary, and thyme,
Where no water sprung, nor a drop of rain fell,
And then she shall be a true love of mine.

"Tell her to dry it on yonder thorn,
Savoury sage, rosemary, and thyme,
Which never bore blossom since Adam was born,
And then she shall be a true love of thine."

"O, will you find me an acre of land,
Savoury sage, rosemary, and thyme,
Between the sea foam, the sea sand,
Or never be a true lover of mine.

"O, will you plough it with a ram's horn,
   Savoury sage, rosemary. and thyme,
And sow it all over with one peppercorn,
   Or never be a true lover of mine.

"O, will you reap it with a sickle of leather,
   Savoury sage, rosemary, and thyme,
And tie it all up with a peacock's feather,
   Or never be a true lover of mine.

"And when you have done and finished your work,
   Savoury sage, rosemary, and thyme,
You may come to me for your cambric shirt,
   And then you shall be a true lover of mine."

MY TRUE LOVE ONCE HE COURTED ME.

OF the following song, the plaint of a broken-hearted girl, I
      have been enabled to obtain four different tunes, all set to
separate verses, but I have found great difficulty in getting the entire
ballad complete.   I at last obtained it from Mr. Halliday, of Newton-
dale, in North Yorkshire, along with the first air here presented.

MY TRUE LOVE ONCE HE COURTED ME.

My true love once he court-ed me, And stole a - way my li - ber-
ty ; He stole my heart with my free goodwill, I must confess I love him still.

My true love once he courted me,
   And stole away my liberty ;
He stole my heart with my free good will,
   I must confess I love him still.

There is an alehouse in this town,
   Where my love goes and sits him down ;
He takes another girl on his knee—
   O ! isn't that a grief to me.

A grief to me, I'll tell you why—
  Because she has more gold than I ;
Her gold will waste, her beauty blast,
  Poor girl, she'll come like me at last.

O, once I [had no cause for woe],
  My love followed me through frost and snow ;
But [ah ! the changes time doth bring]—
  My love passes by and he says nothing.

I wish my baby it was born,
  Set smiling on its nurse's knee ;
And I myself was in my grave,
  And the green grass growing over me.

I wish, I wish, but it's all in vain,
  I wish I were [but free again ;
But free again I'll never be],
  Till an apple grows on an orange tree.

There is a bird in yon churchyard,
  They say it's blind and cannot see ;
I wish it had been the same with me,
  Ere I joined my true love's company.

The next version of the air I got from the remembrance of Mr. Holgate, and his air is also known by several other Leeds people. It is sung to the second verse,

MY TRUE LOVE ONCE HE COURTED ME.

(Second Version.)

There is an ale-house in this town Where my love
goes and sits him down ; He takes another one on his
knee : . . . Don't you think that's a grief to me?

The third and fourth sets are from Mr. Charles Lolley, who heard them sung in his youth near Howden, in the East Riding.

MY TRUE LOVE ONCE HE COURTED ME.

(Third Version.)

A rich young farm - er court - ed me, He stole my heart and li - ber - ty; He stole my heart with my free good - will, I must con - fess I love him still.

The variation in the first line will be noticed.—"A rich, young farmer courted me." Sometimes it is also sung, "A sailor once he courted me." The fourth set of the air is thus, and is sung to the last verse :—

MY TRUE LOVE ONCE HE COURTED ME.

(Fourth Version.)

There is a bird in yon - der tree, They say it is blind and can - not see: I wish it had been the same with me Ere my false lo - ver de - ceiv - ed me.

All the above sets are, I believe, early specimens of melody, and are all also very quaint and well suited to the subject of the song. One of the verses has been taken either by the original writer or is an interpolation from the old Scottish song, "O Waly, Waly, up yon Bank,"

GREEN BUSHES.

I N 1845 Mr. J. B. Buckstone first produced his popular drama, "Green Bushes." There had long been sung, both in England and in Ireland, a ballad bearing this title, and snatches of it were introduced into the play. These fragments were sung by Mrs. Fitzwilliam to an air which was doubtless one of the common tunes for the ballad; it is to be seen in *Duncombe's Musical Casket*, and in other collections.

It is quite different, however, to the following air, which is certainly of a much earlier date. I am indebted for it to Mrs. Holt, of Alderhill, Meanwood, who remembers it being sung in Stockport about 1838. I have also many times met with the same air in the North Riding of Yorkshire, but it has not, to my knowledge, been before printed. The ballad sung to this tune is the same (with an additional verse and some slight verbal differences) with the one in the play.

GREEN BUSHES.

As I was a walking one morning in May,
To hear the birds whistle and see the lambs play ;
I spied a young damsel, so sweetly sang she,
Down by the green bushes where she chanced to meet me.

I stept up to her and thus I did say,
" How far are you going to wander this way ? "
" I'm in search of my true love," the damsel said she,
" Down by the green bushes, where he vowed to meet me."

" I'll buy you fine beavers and fine silken gowns,
I'll buy you fine petticoats, flounced down to the ground,
If you will prove loyal and constant to me ;
Forsake your own true love and marry with me."

" I want none of your beavers, nor none of your hose.
I am not so poor as to marry for clothes,
But if you'll prove constant and true unto me,
I'll forsake my own true love and marry with thee.

" Come, let us be going, kind sir, if you please,
Come, let us be going from under these trees,
For yonder he's coming, my true love, I see,
Down by the green bushes, where he thinks to meet me."

But when he got there, and found she was gone,
He stood like a lambkin that was all forlorn ;
" She's gone with some other and forsaken me,
Adieu the green bushes for ever," said he.

" I'll be like other schoolboys, spending my time in play,
I'll never again be led foolish away,
And false-hearted woman shall deceive me no more ;
Adieu the green bushes—it's time to give o'er."

Besides the above, on a broadside printed by H. Disley,
St. Giles's, is another " Green Bushes," wherein the lady proves
true to her lover. In Petrie's *Music of Ireland*, Vol. II., 1882,
an air entitled " Green Bushes " is given, and the ballad set to one
also occurs in *Songs of the West.* Both tunes, however, are
quite distinct from the foregoing and from each other ; they show
that the ballad has had a wide popularity.

THE GOLDEN GLOVE. '

THIS has been much sung in all parts of the country. I have been able to obtain two traditional airs to the song. One (the first) popular in the East Riding, from Mr Lolley; the second from Mrs. Holt.

Christie has the Ballad in his *Traditional Ballad Airs*, with an air as sung in Scotland, but it has no affinity to either of the following.

THE GOLDEN GLOVE.
(First Version.)

A wealth - y young squire of Tam - worth, we hear, He
court-ed a noble - man's daughter so fair; And for to mar-ry her it
was his in-tent, All friends and re - la-tions had given their consent.

A wealthy young squire of Tamworth, we hear,
He courted a nobleman's daughter so fair ;
And for to marry her it was his intent,
All friends and relations had given their consent.

The time was appointed for the wedding day,
A young farmer chosen to give her away ;
As soon as the farmer the young lady did spy,
He inflamed her heart ; "O, my heart !" she did cry.

She turned from the squire, but nothing she said,
Instead of being married she took to her bed ;
The thought of the farmer still run in her mind,
A way for to have him she quickly did find.

Coat, waistcoat, and breeches she then did put on,
And a hunting she went with her dog and her gun ;
She hunted all round where the farmer did dwell,
Because in her heart she did love him full well.

 ·' She oftentimes fired, but nothing she killed,
At length the young farmer came into the field ;
And to discourse with him it was her intent,
With her dog and her gun to meet him she went.

" I thought you had been at the wedding," she cried,
" To wait on the squire, and give him his bride ;"
" No, sir," said the farmer, "if the truth I may tell,
I'll not give her away, for I love her too well."

" Suppose that the lady should grant you her love,
You know that the squire your rival will prove ;"
" Why, then," said the farmer, " I'll take sword in hand,
By honour I'll gain her when she shall command."

It pleasèd the lady to find him so bold,
She gave him a glove that was flowered with gold,
And told him she found it when coming along,
As she was a hunting with her dog and gun.

The lady went home with a heart full of love,
And gave out a notice that she'd lost a glove ;
And said, " Who has found it, and brings it to me,
Whoever he is, he my husband shall be."

The farmer was pleased when he heard of the news,
With heart full of joy to the lady he goes :
" Dear, honoured lady, I've picked up your glove,
And hope you'll be pleased to grant me your love."

" It's already granted, I will be your bride,
I love the sweet breath of a farmer," she cried ;
" I'll be mistress of my dairy, and milking my cow,
While my jolly brisk farmer is whistling at plough."

And when she was married she told of her fun,
How she went a huntiug with her dog and gun :
" And now I've got him so fast in my snare,
I'll enjoy him for ever, I vow and declare !"

The second version, from Mrs. Holt, is : —

THE GOLDEN GLOVE.

(Second Version.)

A wealth - y young squire of Tam - worth, we hear, He
court - ed a no - ble - man's daughter so fair, And for to mar - ry it
was his in - tent: All friends and re - la - tions had given their consent.

———•———

THE SPINNING WHEEL.

THE distaff and the spinning wheel were favourite instruments with song writers of the last century, both English and Scottish.

Among the old Scotch songs we find many domestic ditties of which they are the theme; as, "The Rock and the Wee Pickle Tow," "The Weary Pound o' Tow," "The Cardin' O't," etc. The English song makers, however, were much more artificial in taste than the writers of these songs, for, instead of singing of the homely side of the subject, they in general pictured a rustic beauty (to whom they gave a classic name), sitting at her cottage door, her charms making some fine gentleman vow he would forsake his town life to live with her in peaceful retirement.

The present song is from the singing of my grandfather, who must have known it in the last century, and I have never been able to meet with anyone who knew the tune as handed down traditionally in the family. The words of the song are to be found in D'Urfey's *Pills to Purge Melancholy*, Vol. II., 1719, and possibly also in the earlier editions. An air is there given to it which is not the same as this now noted down.

The song itself is long, so only a portion of the words are here
reprinted.

THE SPINNING WHEEL.

Up - on a sun - shine, sum - mer's day, When ev - 'ry tree was
green and gay, The morn-ing blush'd with Phœ-bus' ray Just then as-cend-ing
from the sea; As Sil - via did a hunt - ing ride, A
love - ly cot - tage he es - pied, Where love - ly Clo - e
spin-ning sat, And still she turned her wheel a - bout.

Upon a sunshine, summer's day,
When ev'ry tree was green and gay;
The morning blush'd with Phœbus' ray,
Just then ascending from the sea;
As Silvia did a hunting ride,
A lovely cottage he espied,
Where lovely Cloe, spinning, sat,
And still she turned her wheel about.

Her face a thousand graces crown,
Her curling hair was lovely brown,
Her rolling eyes all hearts did win,
And white as down of swans her skin;
So taking her plain dress appears,
Her age not passing sixteen years;
The swain lay sighing at her foot,
But still she turned her wheel about,

"Thou sweetest of thy tender kind,"
Cries he, "this ne'er can suit thy mind ;
Such grace, attracting noble loves,
Was ne'er designed for woods and groves.
Come, come with me to Court my dear,
Partake my love and honour there,
And leave this rural, sordid rout,
And turn no more thy wheel about."

At this, with some few modest sighs,
She turns to him her charming eyes ;
"Ah ! tempt me, sir, no more," she cries,
"Nor seek my weakness to surprise ;
I know your arts to be believed,
I know how virgins are deceived ;
Then let me thus my life wear out,
And turn my harmless wheel about."

. . . .

His cunning tongue so played its part,
He gained admission to her heart ;
And now she thinks it is no sin,
To take love's fatal poison in ;
But, ah ! too late she found her fault,
For he her charms had soon forgot,
And left her e'er the year ran out,
In tears to turn her wheel about.

THE BANKS OF SWEET DUNDEE.

THIS has been popular in nearly every district in England,
and in a number of places in Scotland as well. Though
sublime doggrel, the song is even now a great favourite with the old
folk who still remember it. Perhaps this is on account of the good
air to which the song is set.

For the present copy of the air I am in the first instance obliged
to Mr. Benjamin Holgate, of Leeds ; but I have met with the same,
almost note for note, in Scotland, in North and other parts of
Yorkshire, and in Berkshire. Another Yorkshire termination is
appended.

Christie, in *Traditional Ballad Airs*, gives a set of the air totally different to the one here printed.

The words are frequently met with on broadsides, and the one following the music are from a Catnach ballad sheet.

THE BANKS OF SWEET DUNDEE.

It's of a farmer's daugh . ter, So beau - ti - ful I'm told, Her fa - ther died and left her Five hun - dred pound, in gold. She liv - ed with her un - cie, The cause of all her woe, But you soon shall hear this maid-en fair Did prove his o - ver-throw.

(Another termination.)

woe, And this maid - en fair, as you shall hear, did prove his o - ver-throw.

It's of a farmer's daughter, so beautiful, I'm told,
Her father died and left her five hundred pounds in gold !
She lived with her uncle, the cause of all her woe,
But you soon shall hear, this maiden fair did prove his overthrow.

Her uncle had a ploughboy young Mary loved full well,
And in her uncle's garden their tales of love they'd tell ;
But there was a wealthy squire who oft came her to see,
But still she loved her ploughboy on the banks of sweet Dundee.

    .   .   .   .

Her uncle and the squire rode out one summer's day,
"Young William is in favour," her uncle he did say ;
"Indeed, 'tis my intention to tie him to a tree,
Or else to bribe the press-gang on the banks of sweet Dundee.

The press-gang came to William when he was all alone,
He boldly fought for liberty, but there were six to one ;
The blood did flow in torrents ; " Pray, kill me now," said he,
" I would rather die for Mary on the banks of sweet Dundee."

This maid one day was walking, lamenting for her love,
She met the wealthy squire down in her uncle's grove ;
He put his arms around her ; " Stand off, base man," said she,
" You sent the only lad I love from the banks of sweet Dundee."

He clasped his arms around her and tried to throw her down ;
Two pistols and a sword she spied beneath his morning gown ;
Young Mary took the pistols and the sword he used so free,
But she did fire and shot the squire on the banks of sweet Dundee.

Her uncle overheard the noise, and hastened to the ground,
" O, since you've killed the squire, I'll give you your death wound ;"
" Stand off !" then young Mary said, " undaunted I will be,"
The trigger drew and her uncle slew on the banks of sweet Dundee.

A doctor soon was sent for, a man of noted skill,
Likewise came his lawyer for him to sign his will ;
He left his gold to Mary who fought so manfully,
And closed his eyes no more to rise on the banks of sweet Dundee.

Two verses which are not essential to the story have been omitted. There is enough tragedy and injured innocence in the ballad to furnish the plot of a penny novelette.

THROUGH THE GROVE.

EARLY in the century, " Through the Grove" used to be sung at villages near Leeds, and I have not been able to hear of the song in any other district. The air is a fine one, and is sung by one singer as a solo, the rest of the company singing the two terminal bars of each strain as chorus.

THROUGH THE GROVE.

As through the grove young Johnny did pass, He met Miss Mol - ly,

"Come my lass," And took her by the hand, And took her by the

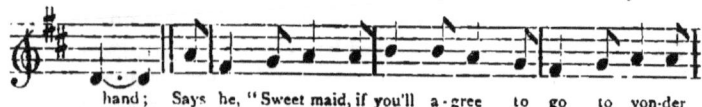

hand; Says he, "Sweet maid, if you'll a - gree to go to yon-der

grove with me, Oh! there we'll have some se ri - ous talk, We'll take a sweet com-

modious walk, And you shall be my bride, And you shall be my bride!"

—As through the grove young Johnny did pass,
He met Miss Molly; "Come, my lass,"
And took her by the hand.

CHORUS.
And took her by the hand.

Said he, "Sweet maid, if you'll agree,
To go to yonder grove with me,
O, there we'll have some serious talk,
We'll take a sweet, commodious walk,
And you shall be my bride."

CHORUS.
And you shall be my bride.

This blushing maid made this reply,
"I fear young men are gien to lie,
I dare not gie consent.

CHORUS.
I dare not gie consent.

" If through the grove with you I go,
And on you should my heart bestow ;
When you had found a fairer maid,
For her you'd quit me, I'm afraid,
And leave me to lament."

CHORUS.
And leave me to lament.

Ballad writers have always been fond of grandiloquent language, and it is most probable that the charming expression, *Commodious* walk, has originally stood *Umbrageous* walk.

The story is told of a farmer lad who at a Methodist Chapel, on the occasion of a new hymn being sung, was observed to join in lustily, although the unfamiliar melody baffled most of the congregation. "'Tha seemed to knaw t' hymn, lad," said one of them to him. "Hymn?" replied the boy; "Why, I thowt they were all singing 'Through the Grove.'"

COME ALL YE BOLD YOUNG COUNTRYMEN.

A N air current in Yorkshire, preserved by Mr. Holgate, only a very imperfect fragment of the words being known.

COME, ALL YE BOLD YOUNG COUNTRYMEN.

Come, all ye bold young countrymen, A warning take by me!

FORTY MILES.

THIS is a good song, and was very popular in Yorkshire in former years. I here print three different sets of the tune, sufficiently alike to show the changes that oral transmission makes in an air. Although it is by no means the same piece, the theme is that with the old Scottish song, "Let me in this ae Night." The tune, of course, bears no affinity to the Scotch one.

The first version following is as it was sung in Leeds and district as Mr. Holgate and others remember it.

FORTY MILES.

It's forty miles I've gone to-day,
I spied a cottage on my way,
    Which I never had seen before,
    Which I never had seen before.

I stepped up to that cottage door,
A pretty, fair maid tripped o'er the floor,
    And she cried aloud, "Who's there?"
    And she cried aloud, "Who's there?"

"My dear, it hails, it rains, it blows,
And I've got wet through all my clothes,
    And I pray you, let me in,
    And I pray you, let me in."

"Oh, no ! kind sir, that never can be,
For there's no one in the house but me,
And I dare not let you in,
And I dare not let you in."

I turned me round away to go,
When she did sweet compassion bestow,
And she called me back again,
And she called me back again.

We spent that night in sweet content,
And the very next morning to church we went,
And I made her my lawful bride,
And I made her my lawful bride.

The second version of the air hereunder is from the singing of
Mr. A. Wardill, of Goathland, Yorkshire, the words being the same.

FORTY MILES.
(Second Version.)

It's for - ty miles I've been to-day; I spied a cot - tage
by the way Which I ne - ver had seen be - fore, ...
. . . . Which 1 ne - ver had seen be - fore.

The third setting is also from Goathland, from Mr. Neswell
Pennock's remembrance.

FORTY MILES.
(Third Version)

It's for - ty miles I've been to-day; I spied a cot - tage by the way
Which I ne-ver had seen be - fore, . . Which I ne-ver had seen be - fore.

I have never seen the words in print, either on a broadside or
elsewhere.

MY VALENTINE.

M R. LOLLEY supplies the tune from the Howden district, and the words are found on ballad sheets. The tune is striking, and has a pleasant flow with it, but in some places it appears to have had modern phrasing embodied among the old. It has, however, certainly been in the state it now is for thirty or forty years.

MY VALENTINE.

Oh! it hap-pen-ed to be one Va-len-tine day, One morn-ing so ear-ly be-time, That a pret-ty, pret-ty maid came to my bed-side, And she want-ed to make me her va-len-tine, . . . And she want-ed to make me her va-len-tine.

O! it happened to be one Valentine Day,
  One morning so early betime,
That a pretty, pretty maid came to my bedside,
  And she wanted to make me her valentine.

· · · · · · · · · · ·

The reader must be content with the first verse ; the whole song is poor doggrel.

THE NIGHTINGALE.

A LSO from Mr. Lolley's singing. The words are but a fragment, and we have not been able to recover more than the two verses here presented. The tune is certainly old.

THE NIGHTINGALE.

My love was a rich farm-er's son When first my ten - der heart he won ; His

love to me he did re - veal I lit - tle thought of the Night in-gale.

My love was a rich farmer's son,
When first my tender heart he won ;
His love to me he did reveal,—
I little thought of the " Nightingale."

That very night my love was lost,
Appeared to me a deadly ghost,
His hair erect and visage pale—
"Thy love was drown'd in the ' Nightingale.' "

. . . .

THE GOWN OF GREEN.

A N air, apparently old, sent to me by Mr. Charles Lolley, who heard it many years ago in the East Riding of York-shire. The words are from a broadside. The old English songs have frequent allusions to wearing the "green gown," just in the same manner that the Scotch ones speak of the loss of the snood, and of the " bonny broom."

THE GOWN OF GREEN.

As my love and I were a walk - ing to view the
mea - dows a - round, A gath - er - ing sweet flowers as they sprung from the ground, She turned her
head and smi - ling said: "Some - bo - dy here has
been, Or else some charm - ing shep - herd-
ess has won the Gown of Green."

As my love and I were walking to view the meadows around,
A-gathering sweet flowers as they sprung from the ground,
She turned her head, and smiling, said, "Somebody here has been,
Or else some charming shepherdess has won the Gown of Green."

. . . .

"O, Polly, love! O, Polly, love! mind what I write to thee,
And when that you do read it 'twill cause you many a tear;
'Twill cause you many tears, my love, and grieve your heart full sore,
For to relate our story when we left our native shore.

"It was early the next morning, all by the dawn of day,
From New York down to Imos we all did march away;
From New York down to Imos we all did march away,
To fight our own relations in North America.

"Thro' fields of blood we ranged, while cannons loud did roar,
And many a valiant sailor lay bleeding in his gore;
There was many a valiant sailor who on the deck did lay,
Who was both killed and wounded in North America.

" It would grieve your heart with pity for to hear the sailors' wives
Lamenting for their husbands, and the melancholy cries,
The children cried out, ' Mammy, we will make them rue the day,
As they did kill my father in North America.' "

. . . .

This delectable effusion is found upon broadsides, and also in a very scarce song book (small quarto in size), entitled, *The Vocal Library*, dated 1818. The song seems to have been an old one, with verses produced at the time of the last American war grafted on.

———◆———

THE FARMER'S BOY.

EVEN now the popularity of "The Farmer's Boy," is great among country singers. Few, however, sing the song to the same air, and at least two different airs, said to be traditional ones, are to be found published in modern sheet music. The three airs here presented, however, differ widely from these printed copies. ⊙ The first from Mrs. Holt, of Alderhill, learned many years ago on the borders of Lancashire and Yorkshire, is thus :—

THE FARMER'S BOY.

The sun was sunk be - hind yon hill, A - cross yon drear - y moor, When poor and lame a boy there came Up to a farm - er's door.

Can you tell me if here it be That I can find em- ploy, To plough and sow, to reap and mow, And be a farm - er's boy.

The sun had set behind yon hills,
  Across yon dreary moor;
When poor and lame, a boy there came
  Up to a farmer's door:
"Can you tell me if here it be
  That I can find employ,
To plough and sow, and reap and mow,
  And be a farmer's boy?

"My father is dead, and mother is left
  With five children, great and small;
And what is worse for mother still,
  I'm the oldest of them all.
Though little, I'll work as hard as a Turk,
  If you'll give me employ,
To plough and sow and reap and mow
  And be a farmer's boy.

"And if that you won't me employ,
  One favour I've to ask,—
Will you shelter me, till break of day,
  From this cold winter's blast?
At break of day, I'll trudge away
  Elsewhere to seek employ,
To plough and sow, and reap and mow,
  And be a farmer's boy."

"Come, try the lad," the mistress said,
  "Let him no further seek;"
"O, do, dear father!" the daughter cried,
  While tears ran down her cheek;
"He'd work if he could, so 'tis hard to want food,
  And wander for employ;
Don't turn him away, but let him stay,
  And be a farmer's boy."

And when the lad became a man,
  The good old farmer died,
And left the lad the farm he had,
  And his daughter for his bride.
The lad that was, the farm now has,
  Oft smiles, and thinks with joy,
Of the lucky day he came that way,
  To be a farmer's boy.

The second air, from the recollection of Mr. Holgate, of Leeds, appears to lack one of the strains of the melody, and to have been a variation of the above.

THE FARMER'S BOY. *(Second Version.)*

The sun was sunk behind yon hill, A-cross yon dreary moor, When,

poor and lame, a boy there came Up to a farm - er's door.

The third setting is from the East Riding of Yorkshire, favoured me by Mr. C. Lolley.

THE FARMER'S BOY. *(Third Version.)*

The sun was sunk be - hind yon hill, A - cross yon

drear - y moor, When, poor and lame, a boy there

came Up to a farm - er's door ; "Can you tell me," said

he, "if a - ny there be That can give me em-

ploy : To plough, and sow, and reap. and

mow, And be a farm - er's boy ?"

It is noticeable, that while the melodies have such variations, the words themselves are fixed.

They were first published in a collection in Dixon's *Songs of the Peasantry of England.*

—————•◆•—— ——

YOUNG ROGER OF THE VALLEY.

YOUNG Roger of the Valley is from the singing of Mrs. Holt, of Alderhill, Meanwood.

The song itself is an old one, and a version of it is printed in Allan Ramsay's *Tea Table Miscellany*, Vol. IV, and in *The Robin*, 1749.

On early ballad sheets it is entitled, "Roger of the Vale."

Ramsay's version commences :—

> Young Roger of the mill,
>   One morning very soon,
> Put on his best apparel,
>   New hose and clouted shoon ;
> And he a-wooing came,
>   To bonny, buxom Nell,
> "Dear lass," cries he, "could'st fancy me,
>   I like thee wondrous well."

The air here given is certainly of last century origin, but is probably not the original one, for in Daniel Wright's *Second Book of the Flute Master Improved, circa* 1715, there is an air most likely intended for the ballad entitled, "Roger of the Vale," but which has not the slightest resemblance to the traditional version here printed.

YOUNG ROGER OF THE VALLEY.

Young Roger of the valley,
  One morning very soon,
Put on his gay apparel,
  Likewise his Sunday shoon ;
And he would go a-courting,
  To bonny, buxom Nell,
"Adzooks !" cried he, "can'st fancy me,
  For I like thy person well.

"My horses I have dress'd,
  And gi'en them corn and hay,
Put on my best apparel,
  And have come this way ;
Let's sit and chat a while,
  With thee, my bonny Nell ;
Dear lass," cries he, "could'st fancy me,
  I like thee wondrous well."

"Young Roger, you're mistaken,"
  The damsel then reply'd,
"I'm not in such a haste
  To be a ploughman's bride ;

Know I then live in hopes,
　To marry a farmer's son;"
"If it be so," says Hodge, "I'll go,
　Sweet mistress, I have done."

"Your horses you have dress'd,
　Good Hodge, I heard you say,
Put on your best apparel,
　And being come this way;"
"O no, indeed, not I,
I'll neither wait, nor sit, nor prate,
　I've other fish to fry.

"Go, take your farmer's son,
　With all my honest heart;
What tho' my name be Roger,
　That goes at plough and cart?
I need not tarry long,
　I soon may gain a wife:
There's buxom Joan, it is well known,
　She loves me as her life."

"Pray, what of buxom Joan?
　Can't I please you as well?
For she has ne'er a penny,
　And I am buxom Nell;
And I have fifty shillings."
　(The money made him smile)
"O then, my dear, I'll draw a chair,
　And chat with thee a while."

Within the space of half-an-hour,
　This couple a bargain struck,
Hoping that with their money,
　They both would have good luck;
"To your fifty I've forty,
　With which a cow we'll buy;
We'll join our hands in wedlock bands,
　Then who but you and I?"

THE SPRIG OF THYME.

T HE air is an East Riding one, which Mr. Lolley favours me with.

There are several ballads extant in the same strain of allegory. The better known one, "I Sowed the Seeds of Love," is an instance; they appear to date from the latter end of the last century.

The tune is pretty, and, I think, is not much corrupted from its original form.

THE SPRIG OF THYME.

Come, all you pret - ty fair maids That are just in your prime, I would have you weed your gar - dens clear, And let no one steal your thyme.

Come, all you pretty fair maids,
    That are just in your prime ;
I would have you weed your garden clear,
    And let no one steal your thyme.

I once had a sprig of thyme,
    It prospered both night and day ;
By chance there came a false young man,
    And he stole my thyme away.

Thyme is the prettiest flower,
    That grows under the sun ;
It's time that brings all things to an end,
    So now my thyme runs on.

But now my old thyme's dead,
    I've got no room for any new,
For in that place where my old thyme grew,
    Is changed to a running rue.
        . . . . .

It's very well drinking ale,
    And it's very well drinking wine,
But it's far better sitting by a young man's side,
    That has won this heart of mine.

THE SPOTTED COW.

THIS is a pretty rustic song, and both the following airs are, I think, pleasing.

The first version is given to me by Mr. Charles Lolley, and is thus :—

THE SPOTTED COW.

(First Version.)

One morn-ing in the month of May, As from my cot I strayed, Just at the dawn-ing of the day, I met a charm-ing maid; Just at the dawn - ing of the day I met a charm-ing maid.

One morning in the month of May,
  As from my cot I strayed,
Just at the dawning of the day,
  I met a charming maid.

"Good morning, fair maid, whither," said I,
  "So early? tell me, now ;"
The maid replied, "Kind sir," she said,
  "I've lost my spotted cow."

"No more complain, no longer mourn,
  Your cow's not lost, my dear,
I saw her down in yonder bourne ;
  Come, love, I'll show you where."

"I must confess you're very kind,
  I thank you, sir," said she ;
"You will be sure her there to find,
  Come, sweetheart, go with me."

Then to the grove we did repair,
  And crossed the flow'ry dale ;
We hugg'd and kiss'd each other there,
  And love was all our tale.

And in the grove we spent the day,
And thought it passed too soon ;
At night we homeward bent our way,
When brightly shone the moon.

If I should cross the flow'ry dale,
Or go to view the plough,
She comes and calls, " Ye gentle swains,
I've lost my spotted cow."

The second setting of the song was sent to me by an anonymous contributor from Calverley, near Leeds.

THE SPOTTED COW.

(Second Version.)

One morn - ing in the month of May, As from my cot I stray - ed, Just

at the dawn-ing of the day, I met a charming maid ; Just

at the dawn - ing of the day I met a charm-ing maid.

The words are found on broadsides, and are also in *Fairburn's Everlasting Songster, circa* 1825. Both words and tunes appear to be of about the beginning of the century.

————◆————

THE GOOSE AND THE GANDER.

M ANY years ago, this used to be a favourite song round about Leeds, though a very silly one. It must claim the indulgence of the reader more upon the merit of the air than that of the words. Before railways and cheap trips acted as general diffusers of London music hall songs, such like ditties in country districts were common in the kitchens of quiet publichouses, and were in general the exclusive copyright of old fogies who gathered there.

The air is from an old manuscript collection of airs in my possession. It appeared in a series of articles upon old tunes contributed by me to the *Leeds Mercury Weekly Supplement ;* otherwise, it has not been in print so far as I am aware.

THE GOOSE AND THE GANDER.

O! the goose and the gan-der walk'd o - ver the green, O! the goose she went bare-foot for fear of being seen, for fear of being seen, boys, for fear of being seen ; O! the goose she went bare - foot for fear of being seen.

O, the goose and the gander went over the green,
O, the goose she walked barefoit for flay'd o' being seen,
For flay'd o' being seen, boys, for flay'd o' being seen,
And the goose she went barefoit for flay'd o' being seen.

I had a black hen and shoo had a white foit,
And shoo laid an egg in a willow tree roit ;
In a willow tree roit, in a willow tree roit,
And shoo laid a white egg in a willow tree roit.

I need scarcely say that this delightful production would be sung only after a certain stage of conviviality had been reached.

———•◦•———

THREE MAIDENS A MILKING DID GO.

THIS air my friend, Mr. Holgate, remembers being sung in and about Leeds. If not very old it is good, and it could be wished that the succeeding verses to the first (the only one which I have printed), were equally meritorious and more suitable for this work.

THREE MAIDENS A MILKING DID GO.

Three maid-ens a milk-ing did go, Three maidens a milk-ing did go; The

wind it blew high, And the wind it blew low, And it blew these three maidens to and fro.

> Three maidens a milking did go,
> Three maidens a milking did go ;
> The wind it blew high, and the wind it blew low,
> And it blew these three maidens to and fro.

COLIN AND PHŒBE.

WITH the few remaining old-fashioned singers in country places, songs of the type of "Colin and Phœbe" are still favourites. They are a survival of the school of fashionable music and song when Mr. Lampe and Dr. Arne composed, and when Mr. Beard and other singers delighted Vauxhall audiences with these composers' productions. "Colin and Phœbe" used to be sung in Yorkshire, and on the Lancashire and Cheshire borders, in the correct old-fashioned style. It being "A Dialogue," a male and female singer took their respective parts, one as Colin and the other as Phœbe, and put as much archness and tenderness into their performance as the part warranted.

The first set of the air Mrs. Holt remembers being sung in Stockport, about fifty years ago, as follows :—

COLIN AND PHŒBE.

(First Version.)

Well met, my dear-est Phœbe; Oh! why in such haste Thro' the
woods and the mea-dows All day have I chased? In the search of my
fair one, Who does me dis - dain! But I hope you'll reward me For all my long pain; . . . . . . But I
hope you'll re - ward me For all my long pain.

"Well met, my dearest Phœbe, O! why in such haste?
Thro' the woods and the meadows all day have I chased,
In the search of my fair one, who does me disdain !
But I hope you'll reward me for all my long pain."

"Go, go, boldest Colin, how dare you be seen,
With a virgin like me that is scarcely sixteen?
To be seen all alone with a man, I'm afraid,
This world will soon call me no longer a maid."

"Never mind what the world says, it shall all prove a lie
We are not alone, there's a cottage hard by ;
Let them judge of our actions, be cheerful, my dear,
For no harm is intended to my Phœbe, I swear."

"Go, go, boldest Colin, you shall say what you will,
You may lie, swear, or flatter, and try your best skill ;
But before I'll be conquer'd, I'd have you to know,
I'll first die a virgin, so pray let me go."

"O, Phœbe, my charmer ! such thoughts I ne'er had,
I came for to see if to-morrow you'd wed ;
But since you so slight me, I'll bid you adieu,
I'll go seek some other girl kinder than you."

"Stay, stay, dearest Colin, a few moments stay,
I will venture to wed if you mean what you say ;
Let to-morrow first come, love, in church you will find
That the lass you thought cruel will always prove kind."

The second setting was noted down for me by Mr. Lolley from East Riding singers.

COLIN AND PHŒBE.
(Second Version.)

It is singular to turn from these two traditional versions to the original, which I had the good fortune to recently find in a folio musical publication of twenty-four pages, entitled, *The New Ballads sung by Mr. Lowe and Miss Stevenson at Vauxhall, set by Mr. Worgan, Book the 4th, 1755. London : Jn. Johnson.*

It is in this work called "Corydon and Phœbe : a Dialogue," and, although the air differs considerably from either of the foregoing sets, the words have come down to us almost as correctly as the original

CORYDON AND PHÆBE.

A DIALOGUE, sung by Mr. Lowe and Miss Stevenson.
Set by Mr. Worgan, 1755.

Corydon—Well met, dearest Phæbe, ah ! why in such haste ?
The woods and the meadows all day have I trac'd,
In search of my fair one, then nothing remains,
But she to reward me for all my past pains.

Phœbe—Why, how now, bold Corydon, what do you mean,
Should a damsel like me, just turned of nineteen,
Be seen all alone with a man ? I'm afraid,
The world would soon think me no longer a maid.

Corydon—Let 'em think as they please, 'twill all prove a lye,
You are not alone, for chaste Cynthia is by ;
She'll judge of our actions, then drive away fear,
No harm is intended to Phœbe, my dear.

Phœbe—No, no, sublime swain, you may say what you will,
Kneel, lye, swear, and flatter, and try all your skill ;
Before I'll be cozen'd, I'd have you to know,
I'll die first a virgin, so pray let me go.

Corydon—Why, Phœbe, such thoughts I ne'er had in my head,
I meant but to know if to-morrow you'd wed ;
But since you won't hear me, I'll bid you adieu,
And find out some other that's kinder than you.

Phœbe—Return, gentle shepherd, a few moments stay,
I'll venture to yield if you mean what you say ;
Let to-morrow then come, at church you shall find,
That she you think cruel yet still may be kind.

It is somewhat amusing to note the change of the word *Cynthia* to *cottage ;* the first-named being doubtless an incomprehensible expression to most of the singers of the song.

***

MARY ACROSS THE WILD MOOR.

I AM in the first instance indebted for the air to this to Mr. Holgate's memory ; but I have found that the song is known in the North and East Ridings to the same tune. Both air and song appear to be not much earlier than the beginning of the present century.

It is often seen on ballad sheets of this and of later date.

MARY OF THE MOOR.

It was one win-ter's night, when the wind It blew bit-ter across the bleak moor, When poor Ma-ry she came with her child, Wand'ring home to her own father's door.

It was one winter's night, when the wind
It blew bitter across the bleak moor,
When poor Mary she came with her child,
Wand'ring home to her own father's door.

She cried—" Father, O pray, let me in,
Do come down and open your own door,
Or the child at my bosom will die,
With the wind that blows on the wild moor.

' Why ever did I leave this cot,
  Where once I was happy and free,
Doomed to roam without friend or a home,
  O ! father have pity on me."

But her father was deaf to her cry,
  Not a voice nor a sound reached the door,
But the watch dog's bark and the wind
  That blew bitter across the wild moor.

Now, think what her father he felt,
  When he came to the door in the morn,
And found Mary dead, and her child
  Fondly clasped in its dead mother's arms.

Wild and frantic he tore his grey hairs,
  As on Mary he gazed at the door,
Who on the cold night there had died,
  By the wind that blew on the wild moor.

Now, her father in grief pined away,
  The poor child to its mother went soon,
And no one lived there to this day,
  And the cottage to ruin has gone.

The villagers point to the cot
  Where a willow droops over the door,
They cry out there poor Mary died,
  With the wind that blew o'er the wild moor.

THE GREY MARE.

THE following was first obtained from my mother, who heard the song sung at Otley, in Yorkshire, about the year 1826-27.

I have since found it is also current among old people in other parts of the country.

Mr. Lolley sends me the air as an elderly relative of his had heard it sung in the East Riding. I also find by a copy of the song to a different air, in *Songs of the West*, that it is known in the West of England.

The East Riding version is :—

THE GREY MARE.

Young Ro-per, the mil-ler, he court-ed of late A farmer's fair daughter called

Beau - ti - ful Kate, For she to her for-tune had five hun-dred pounds, Be-

side rings and jew - els, Be - side rings and jew - els and ma - ny fine gowns.

Young Roger the miller he courted of late,
A farmer's fair daughter called beautiful Kate ;
For she to her fortune had five hundred pounds,
Besides rings and jewels, and many fine gowns.

This glittering money, and beauty likewise,
It tickled his fancy and dazzled his eyes ;
Which caused young Roger to tell his mind,
Unto his own true love that proved constant and kind.

The day being appointed, the money paid down,
It was a fine fortune was five hundred pounds ;
" But," says he, " though your daughter be charming and fair,
I won't have your daughter without the grey mare."

" Oh then," says the farmer, " there's nothing the worse,
My money can soon be put back in my purse ;"
So the money was banished right out of his sight,
And so was Miss Kitty his joy and delight.

And Roger, that rascal, was turned out of door,
They bade him be sure for to come there no more ;
Which caused young Roger for to tear his hair,
And wish he had never stood for the grey mare.

Then about two years after, or a little above,
Young Roger he met with Miss Kitty his love ;
When smiling, said Roger, "Why don't you know me ?"
" If I arn't mistaken I've seen you," said she ;

" For a man in your likeness with long yellow hair,
Did once come a courting my father's grey mare."
" Oh no," said young Roger, "it's that I'll disclaim,
For it was unto you that a courting I came."

" Oh no," says Miss Kitty, " I'll also deny,
And the truth of the matter I will testify,
For unto my father you did solemnly swear,
You would not have his daughter without the grey mare."

I am indebted for another copy of the words to a correspondent,
Mr. C. Butteriss, who informs me that his copy is from Leicester-
shire. It is so similar to Mr. Lolley's version, that it is only here
reproduced in order to show the general accuracy of oral tradition
in transmitting such things down to our own time.

THE GREY MARE.

(Second Version of the Words)

Young Roger the miller he courted of late,
A farmer's gay daughter called beautiful Kate ;
She had to her fortune some five hundred pounds,
Besides handsome jewels and many fine gowns ;
She had to her portion both jewels and rings,
She had to her portion a many fine things.!

The glittering money, and beauty likewise,
Did tickle his fancy and dazzle his eyes ;
Which caused young Roger for to tell his mind,
And unto his lover be constant and kind ;
That no other woman should ere be his bride,
For thou art my jewel, my jewel and pride.

The wedding made ready, the money put down,
A very fine portion, just five hundred pounds ;
" If there is nothing more that falls to my share,
I will not have your daughter without the grey mare ;
If there is nothing more that falls to my share,
I will not have your daughter without the grey mare."

The old farmer made answer unto him with speed,
" Well, I thought you'd have married my daughter indeed ;
But as it so happens my daughter's no worse,
And the money again shall go into my purse ;
But as it is so with you I solemnly swear,
You shall not have my daughter nor yet the grey mare.'

Then Roger, that rascal, was turned out of door,
And bid to begone and come there no more ;
Then Roger he tore his locks of long hair,
And he wished he'd never staid for the grey mare ;
Then Roger he tore his locks of long hair,
And he wished he'd never staid for the grey mare.

In six months hereafter, or something above,
He chanced for to meet with sweet Kitty his love ;
Then smiling, said Roger, " Why don't you know me ? "
" Well, if I'm not mistaken, I've seen you," said she,
" Or one very like you with long yellow hair,
Did once come a courting my father's grey mare."

Then smiling, said Roger, " You are much to blame,
For it was unto you that a courting I came ;
I thought your old father would make no dispute,
In giving his daughter and the grey mare to boot ;
But now he has lost a most dutiful son,
And I'm very sorry for what I have done."

" Oh ! as to thy sorrows I value them not,
For there's plenty of men in this world to be got ;
There's not many young men when at the last fair,
Does marry a wife for the sake of a mare ;
For the price of a mare is not very great,
So fare thee well, Roger, go, man, to thy fate."

ROBIN TAMSON'S SMIDDY.

THE words of this song are well known to Scotchmen, and united to the tune it is frequently heard at convivial meetings. Though so popular, I have never been able to hear of a copy of this air being in print ; it has a similarity to the well-known one, entitled, "The Drummer;" or, "The Piper o' Dundee," but it cannot by any means be said to be the same with it. There is reason to believe that the original name for the present tune of "Robin Tamson's Smiddy," is "Corn Clips," as it was to this tune that Alexander Rodgers (who wrote the words) adapted them. The song "Corn Clips" commenced with the same first line that Rodgers' song does ; but as it was an old ditty, having more humour than delicacy, it is not now known, and possibly never got further into print than on broadsides.

"Robin Tamson's Smiddy" is excellent as a humorous song ; it appeared in the third series of *Whistle-Binkie,* 1842, under the title "My Auld Breeks, air, The Corn Clips."

ROBIN TAMSON'S SMIDDY.

My mith-er men't my auld breeks. And wow! but they were dud-dy; And sent me to get Mal-ly shod At Rob-in Tam-son's smid-dy. The smid-dy stands be-sides the burn, That wimples through the clachan, I ne-ver yet gae by the door, But, aye! I fa' a laugh-ing.

My mither men't my auld breeks,
  An' wow ! but they were duddy,
And sent me to get Mally`shod
  At Robin Tamson's smiddy ;
The smiddy stands besides the burn
  That wimples through the clachan,
I never yet gae by the door,
  But aye I fa' a-laughin'.

For Robin was a walthy carle,
  An' had ae bonnie dochter,
Yet ne'er wad let her tak a man,
  Tho' mony lads had sought her ;
But what think ye o' my exploit ?
  The time our mare was shoeing,
I slippit up beside the lass,
  And briskly fell a-wooing.

An' aye she e'ed my auld breeks,
  The time that we sat crackin',
Quo' I, "My lass, ne'er mind the *clouts*,
  I've new anes for the makin';
But gin ye'll just come hame wi' me,
  An' lea' the carle, your father,
Ye'se get my breeks to keep in trim,
  Mysel, an' a' thegither."

"'Deed, lad," quo' she, " your offer's fair,
  I really think I'll tak' it,
Sae gang awa', get out the mare,
  We'll baith slip on the back o't ;
For gin I wait my father's time,
  I'll wait till I be fifty ;
But na !—I'll marry in my prime,
  An' mak' a wife most thrifty."

Wow ! Robin was an angry man,
  At tyning o' his dochter ;
Thro' a' the kintra-side he ran,
  An' far an' near he sought her;
But when he cam' to our fire-end,
  An' fand us baith thegither,
Quo' I, "Gudeman, I've ta'en your bairn,
  An' ye may tak' my mither."

Auld Robin girn'd an' sheuk his pow,
  "Guid sooth !" quo' he, "you're merry,
But I'll just tak' ye at your word,
  An' end this hurry-burry."
So Robin an' our auld wife
  Agreed to creep thegither ;
Now, I hae Robin Tamson's pet,
  An' Robin has my mither.

HIGHLAND MARY.

WHEN Burns wrote his song, "Highland Mary," he adapted
it to the old air, *Katherine Ogie*, to which it is now always
found united. It was first published with the music in George
Thomson's collection, and Burns in a letter to this gentleman,
dated November 14th, 1792, mentions what poor stuff the song,
Katherine Ogie, is, and how fruitlessly he has tried to mend it, but
thinks that the enclosed—Highland Mary—"is in his happiest
manner," etc.*

The air which is here printed is not *Katherine Ogie*, but one (and
a very sweet one) which was sung early in the present century in
the streets of Leeds to Burns' verses.

It is apparently Scottish, but a very diligent search through
Scottish music collections has failed to bring any tune resembling
it to light. The air is from the singing of my mother, and is also
remembered by another elderly lady. They sang to it two traditional
verses (which are certainly *not* by Burns), these I have met with on
a broadside copy of the song. Burns' verses are so well known
that they do not need repetition, and are here omitted save the
first ; the additional ones follow it.

---

*As Burns says, the original song, *Katherine Ogie, is* poor stuff. In its first form it is found
in *The Merry Musician, or a Cure for the Spleen,* 1716, and afterwards in Ramsay's *Tea Table
Miscellany.* Previously, however, two versions are found in D'Urfey's *Pills,* Vol. II. and VI.,
1719, as *Bonny Katherine Loggy,* and in 1686 the tune is in Playford's *Dancing Master,* as
Lady Catherine Ogle, a New Dance,

HIGHLAND MARY.

Ye banks, and braes, and streams a-round The Cas · tle o' Mont-
gom - er - y, Green be your woods, and fair your flowers, Your
wa - ters ne - ver drum - lie; There sim - mer first un-
fauld her robes, And there the lan - gest tar - ry; For
there I took my last fare-well of my sweet High-land Ma - ry.

Ye banks and braes and streams around
    The castle o' Montgomery,
Green be your woods and fair your flowers,
    And your waters never drumlie ;
There, simmer first unfald her robes,
    And there the langest tarry,
For there I took the last farewell
    O' my sweet, Highland Mary.

    *   *   *   *   *   *   *

All in the silent hour of night,
    Through the green churchyard I'll wander,
Right hearty well I know the spot,
    Where Mary she lies under ;
I'll weep it o'er with silent grief,
    I'll sit and ne'er be weary,
For pleasure there is none for me,
    Without sweet, Highland Mary.

And round sweet Highland's Mary's grave,
   I'll plant the fairest lily,
The primrose sweet, and violet blue,
   Likewise the daffodilly ;
But since the world is grown so wild,
   In the wilderness I'll tarry ;
Come welcome death, thou friend true,
   I'll sleep with Highland Mary.

The following is the East Riding version of "Highland Mary," which will be perceived is but a variatlon from the foregoing set. Mr. Lolley noted it down from his mother's singing.

HIGHLAND MARY.

(Second Version.)

Ye banks and braes, and streams a - round The cas - tle o' Mont-gom - e - ry, Green be your woods and fair your flowers, Your wa - ters ne - ver drum-lie. There sim - mer first un-fauld her robes, And there the lang - est tar - ry ; For there I took the last fare - weel O' my sweet High - land Ma - ry.

THE BREWER LADDIE.

THE air for this ballad was communicated to me by my friend, Mr. Washington Teasdale, who heard it with a fragment of the words something like forty years ago, at a harvest-home supper at Brough, in Westmoreland.

Since Mr. Teasdale gave me the air, I have found the whole
ballad in a reprinted old Glasgow chap book, the original dating
perhaps from the last century.   The air appears of fairly early
date, but is more suggestive of an English military marching tune
than that to a Scottish ballad.   One can almost fancy the shrill
notes of the fifes ringing in the ears.

The air was contributed by me to the *Leeds Mercury Weekly
Supplement*, in a series of articles entitled *Old Tunes*.

THE BREWER LADDIE.

In Perth there liv'd a bon-ny lad, A brew-er to his trade—O, And

he has court-ed Peg-gy Roy, A young and a hand-some maid— O.

With a Fol dol did-dle, &c.

In Perth there lived a bonny lad,
    A brewer to his trade, O ;
And he has courted Peggy Roy,
    A young and a handsome maid, O.
        With a fol dol diddle, etc.

He courted her for seven long years,
    All for to gain her favour ;
But there came a lad out of Edinburgh town,
    Who swore that he would have her.

" O, wilt thou go along with me,
    O, wilt thou go, my honey,
And wilt thou go along with me,
    And leave your own dear Johnnie?"

"O yes, I'll go along with you,
    And along with you I'll ride, O ;
I'll range with you the wide world o'er,
    Tho' I'm to be the brewer's bride, O."

The brewer he came home at e'en,
    Inquiring for his honey,
Her father he made this reply :
    " I've ne'er seen her since Monday."

" Be it not, or be it so,
    Little does it grieve me ;
I'm a young man free, as you can see,
    And a small thing will relieve me.

" There is as good fish in the sea
    As ever yet were taken,
I'll cast my net once o'er again,
    Altho' I am forsaken."

She's rambled up, she's rambled down,
    She's rambled through Kirkaldy,
And many's the time she's rued the day
    She forsook her brewer laddie.

        . . . .

The brewer he set up in Perth,
    And often brewed strong ale, O ;
And he has courted a bonny lass,
    And taken her to his sel', O.

" Ye lover's all, wher'er ye be,
    By me now take a warning,
And never slight your ain true love,
    For fear ye get a waur ane."

THE BANKS OF CLAUDY.

I N Bunting's *Ancient Music of Ireland*, 1840, there is an air
    entitled, " Banks of Claudy," which Bunting noted down from
a harper named Higgins, in 1792, and it is stated to be a very ancient
Irish air ; no words are given. It is very doubtful whether it has
ever been fitted to the ballad here printed; but in Christie's
Traditional Ballad Airs another *Banks of Claudy* is published,
which was obtained from a singer in the North of Scotland, and
with the words nearly the same as the version I print.

The present copy of the song and air I obtained from the singing of a girl in Dumfriesshire, and the tune is totally distinct from either Bunting's or Christie's sets. I am afraid, however, that there is one strain of the melody missing. I can, however, but print the fragment as I have heard it.

The words are supplemented from a London broadside copy.

THE BANKS OF CLAUDY.

'Twas on one sum-mer's morn - ing, All in the month of May, Down by yon flow-'ry gar - den Where Bet - sy did stray, I o - ver - heard a dam - sel In sor - row to com-plain: All for her ab - sent lo - ver Who ploughs the ra - ging main.

'Twas on one summer's morning, all in the month of May,
Down by yon flow'ry garden, where Betsy did stray ;
I overheard a damsel in sorrow to complain,
All for her absent lover who ploughs the raging main.

I went up to this fair maid, and put her in surprise,
I own she did not know me, I being in disguise.
Said I, " My charming creature, my joy and heart's delight,
How far do you travel this dark and rainy night."

" The way, kind sir, to Claudy, if you will please to show,
Pity a maid distracted, for there I have to go ;
I am in search of a faithless young man, and Johnny is his name,
All on the banks of Claudy, I'm told he does remain."

"It's six weeks and better since your true love left the shore,
He is cruising the wide ocean, where foaming billows roar,
He is cruising the wide ocean for honour and gain,
I was told the ship was wreck'd off the coast of Spain."

When she heard the dreadful news, she fell into despair,
To wringing of her hands, and tearing of her hair ;
"Since he is gone and left me, no man on earth I'll take,
In some lonely valley I'll wander for his sake."

His heart was filled with joy, no longer he could stand,
He flew into her arms, saying, "Betsy I'm the man,
I am the faithless young man, whom you thought was slain,
And since we are met on Claudy's bank, we'll never part again."

BRAES OF STRATHBLANE.

T HE air and several of the verses were picked up from the
same girl's singing in Dumfriesshire. The words having
been found since on a ballad sheet.

The air is pecular in structure, and is no doubt an old one.

THE BRAES OF STRATHBLANE.

As I went a walk-ing one fine sum-mer's day, Down
by yon green meadows, I did care-less-ly stray, I spied a fair maid : she was
stand-ing her lane, And was bleaching her claes on the braes of Strathblane.

As I went a walking one fine summer's day,
Down by yon green meadows I did carelessly stray ;
I spied a fair maid, she was standing her lane,
And was bleaching her claes on the Braes of Strathblane.

I stepped up to her as I seemed for to pass,
" You are bleaching your claes, my bonny lass ;
It's a twelvemonth and better since I had you in my mind,
An' for to get married if you would incline."

"To marry ! To marry, lad ! I am too young,
Besides you young men have a flattering tongue ;
My father and mother would angry be,
If I were to marry a rover like thee."

" O haud your tongue, lassie, and do not say so,
You know not the pain that I undergo;
Consent, my dear lassie, for to be my ain,
And we will be happy on the Braes of Strathblane."

"O tempt me no longer," this fair maid did say,
"You would be far better to go on your way ;
I'd not think myself happy to stay here my lane,
Nor with you pass my life on the Braes of Strathblane."

This young man turned round with the tear in his e'e,
" I wish you good morning, young lassie," said he ;
" I wish you good morning as we are here our lane,
I'll go court another on the Braes of Strathblane."

" O stay awhile, laddie, you've quite won my heart,
For here is my hand, love, we never shall part ;
No, we never shall part till the day that we die,
May all good attend us wherever we be."

" O now you've consented, but it is out of time,
Since the last word you spoke I have altered my mind ;
The clouds look heavy, I'm afraid we shall have rain,"
So we shook hands and parted on the Braes of Strathblane.

" Now all you pretty fair maids, wherever you be,
Never slight a young man for his poverty ;
For the slighting of young men I'm afraid you'll get nane,
So single I wander on the Braes of Strathblane."

AN AULD MAN HE COURTED ME.

THE miseries of marrying an "auld man" have frequently formed the subject of Scottish song, as instanced by " What can a Young Lassie do wi' an Auld Man," "The Auld Man wi' his Beard new shaven," and others. Even "Auld Robin Gray" may be included in the category, though it is scarcely in the same strain with the two first-named and the one now following.

This, I noted down from the singing of Mr. A. Wardill, of Goathland, in North Yorkshire. The first verse only is here printed. The air is old, and the *Derry Down* chorus comes in quaintly. The burden of every verse is, as in the first, " Maids, while you live never wed an auld man."

AN AULD MAN HE COURTED ME.

An auld man he court - ed me, Hey, der - ry down, der - ry! An
auld man he court-ed me, Hey, derry down! An auld man he court-ed me
All for his bride to be; Maids, while you live never wed an auld man.

An auld man he courted me ;
    Hey derry down, derry.
An auld man he courted me ;
    Hey derry down.
And auld man he courted me,
All for his bride to be ;
    Maids while you live,
    Never wed an auld man.

ROTHER GLEN.

THIS is but a fragment which I heard sung by a native of Dumfriesshire.

The air is I think a good one, and has every appearance of being old.

I much regret that I could not obtain more of the song than the first verse.

ROTHER GLEN.

When I was young in youth did bloom,
Where fancy led me I did roam ;
From town to town, and country round,
And to a place named Rother Glen.

. . . .

THE MAMMY'S PET.

THE Mammy's Pet is but the first verse out of many, and the only one remembered by the person from whom I got the air.

This was Mrs Calvert, of Gilnockie, Dumfriesshire, who first heard it sung by her grandmother, the celebrated Tibbie Shiel. The song promises to have been a humorous one, on the dangers of marrying a girl whose parents have failed to keep their promise with regard to her tocher.

THE MAMMY'S PET.

My fa-ther he promised me hor - ses, My mo-ther she promised me
kye, But when the time was ap - point-ed, The whole of them did deny, The whole of them did de - ny! . . And weel ye may ken
that, That ne-ver a young man af - ter me Will mar ry a mammy's pet!

My father he promised me horses,
My mother she promised me kye;
But when the time was appointed,
The whole of them did deny,
The whole of them did deny!
And weel ye may ken that,
That never a young man after me,
Will marry a mammy's pet.

MAGGIE'S SMILE.

THIS song is contributed by a lady, who heard it in Dunfermline, where it was known many years ago.

The words are certainly not very old—not earlier than 1810 to 1830—but I have been able to find neither the words nor the air in print.

It is not unlikely that they may be recognised and found by a diligent search among the semi-modern Scottish musical publications. While bearing this in mind, I hesitated to omit such a good air and song, deeming sins of omission in this case greater than sins of commission.

MAGGIE'S SMILE.

I hae courted Maggie mony a day,
To tell how long I'd weary, O !
But ne'er a word wad Maggie say,
She wad'na be my dearie, O !

Chorus—But O, her smile, her bonny smile,
Tho' she'd no speak it spak' again,
Tho' she wad say : "gae bide awa ;"
Her smile said, "aye, come back again."

She placed a kebbuck on the shelf,
But fient a knife my Maggie brang ;
She then wi mony a jeering word,
Bade me sit in and talk a whang.
But O, her smile, her bonny smile, etc.

She tried to gloom, but couldna' gloom,
I then grew bold, and spak' again ;
Said she, "Gae whistle on your thumb,
But mind, sir, come nae back again."
But O, her smile, her bonny smile, etc,

> But jeering words and woman's wile,
> Should never mak' a lover shy ;
> I've won my Maggie's bonny smile,
> I've won my Maggie's heart forbye.
> But O, her smile, her bonny smile, etc.

GLOWEROWERUM.

TO the lady who favours me with " Maggie's Smile," I am
also indebted for the following. The remarks respecting
the probability of "Glowerowerum" being a printed air holds
good as in the case of " Maggie's Smile," and I must plead the same
excuse for inserting it in a gathering of traditional airs. The song,
with the air, is from the same source as " Maggie's Smile," and the
air is equally good.

"Glowerowerum" is used as a place-name for a farmhouse in
several parts of the North of England and in Scotland. It
signifies a situation having an extensive prospect.

GLOWEROWERUM.

There lived an auld man at the top 'o the knowes, His legs were nae better than guid os-ier boughs; 'Twad hae set-ted him bet-ter tae hae herded his yowes Than hae taen the tack o' bon-nie Glower-owe - rum.

> There lived an auld man at the top o' the knowes,
> His legs were nae better than guid osier boughs ;
> 'Twad hae setted him better tae hae herded his yowes,
> Than hae ta'en the tack o' bonnie Glowerowerum.
> *Chorus—(The air being repeated.)*

Then whilk o' ye lasses 'll gang to Glowerowerum,
Whilk o' ye lasses 'll gang to Glowerowerum,
Whilk o' ye lasses 'll gang to Glowerowerum,
Tae be the guid wife o' bonnie Glowerowerum?

" Mither, I'm gawn to Lawrence fair,"
" Laddie, what are ye gaun tae do there?"
" I'm gaun tae buy baith harrows and ploughs,
Tae farm the land o' Glowerowerum knowes.
> Then whilk o' ye lasses 'll gang to Glowerowerum, etc.

" I'm no for the lass that says naithing ava,
Nor yet for the lassie that speaks for us a';
I'm no for the lassie that rages and flytes,
And blames the guidman when it's a' her ain wyte.
> Then whilk o' ye lasses 'll gang to Glowerowerum, etc.

" I'm no for the lass wi' the bonnie black locks.
Nor yet for the lass wi' the braw ribbon knots ;
But I'm for the lass wi' the bonnie bank notes,
Tae 'plenish the farm o' bonnie Glowerowerum."
> Then whilk o' ye lasses 'll gang to Glowerowerum, etc.

" Mither, I'm gaun tae Lawrence fair."
" Lassie, what are ye gaun to do there?"
" I'm gaun to buy baith laces and lawn,
Tae wear on my head when I get the guidman."

Chorus—For I am the lassie that's gaun to Glowerowerum,
I am the lassie that's gaun to Glowerowerum,
For though he may be but a weary concern,
It's a braw bonnie tack Glowerowerum farm.

COUPSHAWHOLME FAIR.

THIS lively and picturesque description of a Scotch country fair, I heard sung at Gilnockie, in Dumfriesshire. I was informed that it was the composition of a labouring man, now dead, named Robert Anderson. I am not aware that this song has ever been in print ; it certainly deserves to be better known. Coupshawholme is the local name for Castleton (now called Newcastleton), a small town in Roxburghshire, not far from the borders,

The air to which the song is adapted is assuredly old. The singer prolongs the starting note of each strain to an abnormal length.

COUPSHAWHOLME FAIR.

On a Friday it fell in the month of April,
O'er the hills cam' the morn wi' its blithesomest smile ;
The folks were a' thranging the roads everywhere,
Making haste to be in at the Coupshawholme Fair.

There were seen coming in frae the mountains and glen,
Baith the rosy-faced lasses, and strapping young men :
A' jumping wi' joy, and unburdened wi' care,
And meeting auld freens at the Coupshawholme Fair.

It's a day when auld courtships are often renewed,
A' disputes set aside, or more hotly pursued ;
What Barleycorn Johnny sees fit to declare
Is law, for he's king at the Coupshawholme Fair.

There's pethirs* and potters, and gingerbread stands,
Peep-shows, puff and dart men, and big caravans ;
There's fruit frae a' nations exhibited there,
And kail plants frae Hawick at the Coupshawholme Fair.

There's lads for the lasses, and toys for the bairns,
Auld blin' ballant singers, and folks wi' nae arms ;
The fiddler is here, and the tumbler there,
Wi' nut-men and spice-men at Coupshawholme fair.

* Pedlars.

Now next is the hiring, if you want to hear tell,
I'll tell it as far as I've seen it mysel';
What wages are gien is ill to declare,
Sae muckle they vary at Coupshawholme Fair.

The first I saw hired was a strapping young quean,
He asked her her age and where she had been ;
What wages she wanted, and how long she'd been there,
An' gin she wad hire at the Coupshawholme Fair.

. . . .

The memory of my informant here failed him, and I have not
been able to recover the succeeding verse or verses.

AS WE WERE A-SAILING.

THIS fragment was obtained on the Yorkshire coast. It must
be of some degree of antiquity as it relates to a naval engagement with the Spaniards. It is to be noticed that a vessel
called the " Rainbow" (as in this ballad) is also immortalized in
ballad, relating to "A Famous Sea Fight between Captain Ward
and the Rainbow."

Ward was a noted pirate in Queen Elizabeth's reign, and the
vessel in question was sent out to destroy Ward's ship. We were
then at war with Spain, and it appears not unlikely that the
" Rainbow" here mentioned is the same vessel.

One verse of Captain Ward runs—

Our Queen she got a ship built, a ship of noble fame,
And she was called the Rainbow—you might have heard her name ;
And she was called the Rainbow, and on the seas went she,
With full five hundred seamen bold to bear her company.

In the second verse of the present song a heroic female suddenly
appears and takes the place of the slain commander. Probably,
some verse now lost would have explained how the damsel turned
up at such an opportune moment. I have not found the ballad in
print.

AS WE WERE A-SAILING.

As we were a-sailing unto the Spanish shore,
Where the drums they did beat, my boys, and the loud cannon did roar,
We spied our lofty enemies come bearing down the main,
Which caused us to hoist our topsails again.

. . . .

Oh ! broadside to broadside, to battle then we went,
To sink one another it was our intent ;
The very second broadside our captain he got slain,
And this damsel she stood up in his place to command.

We fought four hours, four hours so severe,
We scarcely had one man aboard of our ship that could steer ;
We scarcely had one man aboard could fire off a gun,
And the blood from our deck like a river did run.

For quarter, for quarter, those Spanish lads did cry,
" No quarter ! no quarter !" this damsel did reply ;
" You've had the best of quarter that I can afford,
You must fight, sink, or swim, my boys, or jump overboard."

So now the battle's over, we'll take a glass of wine;
And you must drink to your true love, and I will drink to mine ;
Good health unto this damsel who fought all on the main,
And here's to the royal gallant ship called Rainbow by name.

THE BOLD PRIVATEER.

THE air is from Mr. Lolley, picked up in the East Riding of Yorkshire, and the words are found on ballad sheets which are sold in Hull and other seaport towns. The story, of course, dates from at least our last French or American war.

THE BOLD PRIVATEER.

Oh! fare you well, my Pol - ly dear, since you and I must part, In cross-ing of the seas, my love, I'll pledge to you my heart; For our ship she now lies wait - ing, so fare you well, my dear: For I just now am going a - board of a bold pri - va - teer.

"O, fare you well, my Polly dear, since you and I must part,
In crossing of the seas, my love, I'll pledge to you my heart ;
For our ship she now lies waiting, so fare you well, my dear,
For I just now am going aboard of a bold privateer."

She said, " My dearest Jemmy, I hope you will forbear,
And do not leave your Polly in grief and in despair ;
You'd better stay at home with the girl you love so dear,
Than venture on the seas your life in a bold privateer."

" You know, my dearest Polly, your friends they do me slight ;
Besides, you have two brothers would take away my life ;
From them I then must wander, myself to get me clear,
So I am just now going aboard of a bold privateer.

"And when the wars are over, if God does spare our lives,
We will return safe back again to our sweethearts and our wives,
And then I will get married to my charming Polly, dear,
And forever bid adieu to the bold privateer."

ON BOARD OF A MAN-OF-WAR.

THIS is another East Riding tune, which, with the words, is much thought of among the seafaring classes round about Hull. The incident of a girl going to sea disguised in sailor's attire during the last century's naval wars was really not an uncommon one; there are many such recorded. Considering the hard life and the tyranny to which the sailors of that period were subjected, it is a scarcely to be conceived impulse which would force a girl to such a proceeding.

The immortal ballad of " Billy Taylor" chronicles a similar adventure on the part of a young lady of roving proclivities. The comic and well-known version of " Billy Taylor" it may be here noticed is a parody on a more serious effusion (really quite as comic), which appears to narrate a true circumstance.

In the present ballad the line—

" She faced the walls of China where her life was not insured

is a highly poetical flight on the part of the poet, and would be doubtlessly well appreciated by the audience it was intended for.

ON BOARD OF A MAN-OF-WAR.

Young Su-san was a blooming maid, So va - liant, stout, and bold!" And
when her sail - or went a-board, Young Su - san, we are told, Put
on a jol - ly sail - or's dress, And daubed her hands with tar : To
cross the ra - ging seas For love on board of . a Man - of - War.

Young Susan was a blooming maid, so valiant, stout and bold,
And when her sailor went to sea, young Susan, we are told,
Put on a jolly sailor's dress, and daubed her hands with tar,
To cross the raging seas for love, on board of a man-of-war.

It was in Portsmouth harbour this gallant ship was moored,
And when young Susan shipped there were nine hundred men aboard ;
'Twas then she was contented, all bedaubed with pitch and tar,
To be with her sweet William on board of a man-of-war.

When in the Bay of Biscay, she aloft like lightning flew,
Respected by the officers and all the jovial crew ;
In battle she would boldly run, not fearing wound or scar,
And did her duty by her gun, on board of a man-of-war.

She faced the walls of China, where her life was not insured,
And little did young William think his Susan was on board ;
But by a cruel cannon ball she did receive a scar,
And she got slightly wounded, on board of a man-of-war.

When on the deck young Susan fell, of all the whole ship's crew,
Her William was the very first who to her assistance flew ;
She said, " My jolly sailor, I've for you received a scar,
Behold your faithful Susan bold, on board of a man-of-war."

Then William on his Susan gazed with wonder and surprise,
He stood some moments motionless, while tears stood in his eyes,
He cried, " I wish instead of you I had received that scar,
O, love, why did you venture on board of a man-of-war ? "

At length to England they returned, and quickly married were,
The bells did ring, and they did sing, and banished every care !
They often think upon that day when she received that scar,
When Susan followed her true love on board of a man-of-war.

—◆●◆—

JOHNNY TODD.

JOHNNY TODD is a child's rhyme and game, heard and seen
played by Liverpool children.

The air is somewhat pleasing, and the words appear old, though
some blanks caused by the reciter's memo y have had to be filled up.

JOHNNY TODD.

John-ny Todd he took a no-tion For to go a-cross the sea,
And he left his love be-hind him, Weeping by the Li-ver-pool sea.

Johnny Todd he took a notion
For to go across the sea,
And he left his love behind him,
Weeping by the Liverpool sea.

For a week she wept full sorely,
Tore her hair and wrung her hands,
Till she met another sailor
Walking on the Liverpool sands.

"Why, fair maid, are you a-weeping,
For your Johnny gone to sea?
If you'll wed with me to-morrow,
I will kind and constant be.

" I will buy you sheets and blankets,
I'll buy you a wedding ring,
You shall have a gilded cradle
For to rock your baby in."

Johnny Todd came back from sailing,
Sailing o'er the ocean wide ;
But he found his fair and false one,
Was another sailor's bride.

All young men who go a-sailing,
For to fight the foreign foe,
Don't you leave your love like Johnny—
Marry her before you go.

CAPTAIN DEATH.

THIS ballad relates to a fierce engagement between a French
vessel named the "Grand Alexander" from St. Malo, and
an English privateer named the "Terrible," of twenty-six guns and
two hundred men, commanded by Captain Death. The English
ship was captured, but so obstinate was the encounter that (if we

are to believe the ballad) only sixteen of the crew survived; Captain Death and most of the officers being killed. The date of this event was the 23rd of December, 1757.

The words of the ballad are to be found in Ritson's *Select Collection of English Songs*, 1783; in *The Early Naval Ballads of England*, edited by J. O. Halliwell, for the Percy Society, 1841; and in Logan's *Pedlars' Pack of Ballads*, 1869.

The air has not been printed, but I have found it in a small manuscript volume of airs for the violin in my possession, apparently written down about the beginning of the century.

CAPTAIN DEATH.

The Muse with the he-ro's brave deeds being fired, For sim·i-lar views had their

bo·soms in-pired, For free·dom they fought, and for glo·ry con-tend,—The

Muse o'er the he·ro still mourns as a friend; Then, oh! let the Muse this poor

tri·bute be·queath To the true Bri·tish he·ro, the

brave Cap·tain Death, The brave Cap-tain Death, the

brave Cap·tain Death; To a true British hero, the brave Captain Death.

The Muse and the hero together are fired,
The same noble views have their bosoms inspired,
As freedom they love and for glory contend,
The Muse o'er the hero still mourns as her friend;
And here let the Muse her poor tribute bequeath,
To one British hero—'tis brave Captain Death.

His ship was the "Terrible"—dreadful to see,
His crew were as brave and as gallant as he ;
Two hundred or more was their good complement,
And, sure, braver fellows to sea never went ;
Each man was determined to spend his best breath
In fighting for Britian and brave Captain Death.

A prize they had taken, diminish'd their foes,
And soon the good prize ship was lost in her course ;
The French privateer and the "Terrible" met,
The battle begun, all with horror beset ;
No heart was dismayed, each as bold as Macbeth,
They fought for old England and brave Captain Death.

Fire, thunder, balls, bullets were seen, heard, and felt—
A sight that the heart of Bellona would melt ;
The shrouds were all torn, and the decks filled with blood,
And scores of dead bodies were thrown in the flood ;
The flood from the days of old Noah and Seth,
Ne'er saw such a man as our brave Captain Death,

At last the dread bullet came wing'd with his fate,
Our brave Captain dropped, and soon after, his mate ;
Each officer fell, and a carnage was seen,
That soon dyed the waves from crimson to green ;
And Neptune rose up and he took off his wreath,
And gave it a triton to crown Captain Death,

Thus fell the strong "Terrible," bravely and bold,
But sixteen survivors the fate can unfold ;
The French were the victors, though much to their cost,
For many brave French were with Englishmen lost ;
And thus says old Time, "From good Queen Elizabeth,
I ne'er saw the fellow of brave Captain Death."

The first verse united to the music is from a different copy.

----♦----

OUTWARD BOUND.

A SAILOR'S chanty, known at many ports to the accompany-
ing tune. The air was picked up from sailors by Mr.
Charles Lolley (to whom I am indebted for many tunes in this
collection), and the words are from a broadside.

OUTWARD BOUND!

To Liv-er-pool docks we bid a-dieu, To Suke, and Sal, and
Kit-ty too: The an-chor's weigh'd, the sails unfurled, We're bound to cross the
watery world, For we are outward bound; . Hur-rah! we're outward bound!

To Liverpool docks we bade adieu,
To Suke and Sall and Kitty, too ;
The anchor's weigh'd, the sails unfurled,
We're bound to cross the watery world.

CHORUS.

For don't you see we're outward bound,
Huzza ! we're outward bound.

The wind blows from east-nor.-east,
Our ship will sail ten knots at least ;
The purser will our wants supply,
So while we live we'll ne'er say die.
For huzza ! we're outward bound, etc.

And should we touch at Malabar,
Or any other port as far,
Our purser he will tip the chink,
And just like fishes we will drink.
For huzza ! etc.

. . . .

And now we're haul'd into the docks,
When the pretty girls they come in flocks ;
And one unto the other will say,
" Here comes Jack with his three years' pay."
For huzza ! we're homeward bound.

And now we're off to the "Dog and Bell,"
Where good liquors they always sell ;
In comes the landlord with a smile,
Saying, "Drink, lads, drink, it's worth your while,
 For don't you see you're homeward bound," etc.

But when our money is gone and spent,
There's none to be borrowed, nor any to be lent ;
In comes the landlord with a frown,
Saying, "Get up, Jack, let John sit down,
 For don't you see he's homeward bound," etc.

JUST AS THE TIDE WAS FLOWING.

THIS is another old sailors' favourite, noted down for me by
Mr. Lolley. The air is old and much resembles "The Peacock"
—an Irish tune seldom met with, but included in R. A. Smith's *Irish
Minstrel, circa* 1826, and in one of Holden's collections of Irish
Airs, *circa* 1800. The air has much of the characteristics of Scotch
melody. It is also sung to this air in the North Riding. The words
are from a broadside.

JUST AS THE TIDE WAS FLOWING.

One morn-ing in the month of May, Down by a roll-ing

riv - er, A jol - ly sail - or, he did stray, And there be-held a

lov - er; She care-less-ly a - long did stray, A-view-ing of the

daisies gay, She sweetly sang a round-e-lay Just as the tide was flow - ing.

One morning in the month of May,
  Down by a rolling river,
A jolly sailor he did stray,
  And there beheld a lover.
She carelessly along did stray,
  A viewing of the daises gay.
She sweetly sang her roundelay.
  Just as the tide was flowing.

Her dress it was as white as milk,
  And jewels did adorn her skin,
It was as soft as any silk,
  Just like a lady of honour.
Her cheeks were red, her eyes were brown,
  Her hair in ringlets hanging down,
Her lovely brow without a frown,
  Just as the tide was flowing.

I made a bow and said, " Fair maid,
  How came you here so early ;
My heart by you it was betrayed,
  And I could love you dearly.
I am a sailor come from sea,
  If you'll accept my company,
To walk and see the fishes play,
  Just as the tide is flowing."

No more was said, but on her way
  We both did gang together ;
The small birds sang, the lambs did play,
  And pleasant was the weather.
We both being weary sat us down,
  Beneath a tree with branches round :
Then to the church we soon were bound,
  Just as the tide was flowing.

———◆◆———

THE INDIAN LASS.

SAILORS are much given to beguiling the monotony of their voyages by songs, and any one which has a simple and taking air and words, not too high flown, will be acceptable. The old forecastle ditties are, however, passing away on the water like those on the land. Many of the old sailor songs are long, dreary ballads, having for their theme some naval engagement of the last century, or possibly

some dismal account of a shipwreck. Others, again, like the
" Indian Lass," narrate in simple language the joys of a sailor's life
ashore.

Such songs and tunes have had, we may be sure, their birth on
shipboard, and been passed from sailor to sailor. Many interesting
old fragments of this class could be picked up in a voyage in a
trading vessel, or in dock side public houses.

A different and distinct class of airs and songs are the " Chanties,"
such as " Whiskey for my Johnny," " The Rio Grande," and others;
but these are *work*, not *play* songs, for they are used solely for the
purpose of timing the pull of the ropes in working the vessel; the
words of these are generally merely extempore rhymes strung together. Sailors have another song which they sing when a vessel
is paid off. This is one roughly put together describing the character
of the vessel and its officers, and is eagerly listened to by the fresh
hands seeking a berth aboard the vessel.

The " Indian Lass " is found on broadsides, and the first version
of the air I got from a person's singing in North Yorkshire.

THE INDIAN LASS.

As I was a walking on a far distant shore,
I went into an ale-house to spend half-an-hour ;
And as I sat smoking beside of my glass,
By chance there came in a fine young Indian lass.

This lovely young Indian, on the place where she stood,
I viewed her sweet features, and found they were good ;
She was neat, tall, and handsome, her age was sixteen,
She was born and brought up in a place near Orleans.

I sat down beside her and squeezèd her hand,
" I am a poor sailor, not one of this land,
But I will prove constant if you will wed with me,
Then let us be married ere I go to sea."

. . . .

" Kind sir," said this maiden, " I pray you to stay,
You shall have my portion without more delay ;
O, do not go leave me to cross the wide sea,
For I have enough both for you and for me."

The day was appointed that we were to sail,
To cross the wide ocean to leave her a while ;
She says, "When you're over in your own native land,
Remember the young Indian that squeezed your hand."

So early next morning we were going to sail ;
This lovely young Indian on the beach did bewail ;
I took off my hankerchief and wipèd her eyes,—
" O, do not go leave me, my sailor," she cries.

We weighèd our anchor and away then we flew,
A sweet. pleasant breeze parted me from her view ;
But now I am over and taking my glass,
Here is a good health to the young Indian lass.

The following is another set for " The Indian Lass," noted down
by Mr. Lolley.

THE INDIAN LASS.

(Second Version.)

As I was a walk-ing on a far dis-tant shore, I called at an
ale-house to spend half-an-hour : And as I sat smok-ing beside me a glass, By chance there came by a fair In-di-an lass,

THE DROWNED SAILOR.

THE "Drowned Sailor" is a Yorkshire song, which I heard sung at Flamborough, and I have reason to believe it is also known in the district between there and Whitby. The scene of the story is laid near Robin Hood's Bay, six miles south of Whitby; Stowbrow mentioned in the ballad being a large and high tract of land on the south side of the bay. No doubt the circumstance of a girl finding her drowned lover really may have occurred, and hence the ballad.

THE DROWNED SAILOR.

On Stow - brow, on Stow - brow a fair young maid did dwell; She loved a hand-some sail - or, and he lov-ed her quite as well; He pro-mised he would mar - ry her when back he did re - turn, But, ah! what mis-for - tunes the world it does con - tain.

On Stowbrow, on Stowbrow, a fair young maid did dwell,
She loved a handsome sailor and he loved her quite as well ;
He promised he would marry her when back he did return,
But, ah ! what misfortunes the world it does contain.

As they were a-sailing, a-sailing by night,
The moon it was shaded, and dismal was the night ;
The storm it was raging, and the waves the vessel bore,
Till they dashed these poor sailors all on the rocky shore.

Some of them were single, and some of them had wives,
And all of these poor sailor lads had to swim for their lives ;
But this unhappy sailor who tried his life to save,
Instead of being married he found a watery grave.

Now, as she was walking from Stowbrow to Bay,
She saw a drowned sailor that on the sand did lay ;
The nearer she drew to him it brought her to a stand,
She spied it was her true love by the mark upon his hand.

She kissed him, she caressed him, ten thousand times all o'er,
And said, "These awful billows have washed my love ashore ;"
But soon this pretty damsel she lay down by his side,
And in a few moments she kissed him and died.

Now, this couple was buried in Robin Hood's Churchyard,
And for them a memorial stone at their head was raised ;
And all you true lovers that do this way pass by,
Pray shed a tear of pity from out your glistening eye.

THE SUMMER MORNING.

THE "Summer Morning," or, as it is frequently called, "The White Cockade," has been well-known in all parts of Yorkshire, and I have got copies of the air and song from several singers of old songs. Although so popular, the air never seems to have been printed, except a copy contributed by me some years ago to the *Leeds Mercury Weekly Supplement.*

I originally noted it down from the singing of my mother, who heard it sung in Leeds about the year 1820. In J. H. Dixon's *Songs of the Peasantry of England,* 1857, the words are printed as taken down from the recitation of his brother, and the song is stated to have been popular in Durham.

Mr. Dixon states that the air is printed in Chappell's *Popular Music of the Olden Time,* but this is a mistake, for no mention is made of the song in that work, nor is it in the first edition of Chappell's book.

The song itself is apparently of the date of the latter part of the eighteenth century, and as some reference is made to the "Hollanders," may perhaps be more distinctly referred to the period of an expedition to repel French encroachments in Flanders and the Netherlands in 1793. The tune is no doubt older than this date, and may have belonged to an earlier song, now lost or which has changed its tune.

In singing, the words in italics are to be repeated three times.

THE SUMMER MORNING.

It was one summer morning as I went o'er the moss,
I had no thought of 'listing, till the soldiers did me cross ;
They kindly did invite me to a flowing bowl, and down
They advancèd me some money, ten guineas and a crown.

'Tis true my love has 'listed, he wears a white cockade,
He is a handsome, tall young man, besides a roving blade ;
He is a handsome young man, and he's gone to serve the King,
Oh, my very heart is breaking, all for love of him.

My love is tall and handsome, and comely for to see,
And by a sad misfortune a soldier now is he ;
I hope the man that 'listed him may not prosper night or day,
For I wish that the Hollanders may sink him in the sea.

Oh, may he never prosper, oh, may he never thrive,
Nor anything he takes in hand so long as he's alive ;
May the very grass he treads, upon the ground refuse to grow,
Since he's been the only cause of my sorrow, grief, and woe.

Then he pulled out a handkerchief and wiped her flowing eyes,
" Leave off these lamentations, likewise these doleful sighs,
Leave off your grief and sorrow, while I march o'er the plain,
We'll be married, we'll be mar-ri-èd, when I return again."

Oh now my love has 'listed, and I for him will rove,
I'll write his name on every tree that grows in yonder grove ;
Where the huntsman he does hallo, and the hounds do sweetly cry,
To remind me of my ploughboy until the day I die.

A broadside version of the ballad only includes the first, second, fourth, and fifth verses. The first line begins—

"It was one Monday morning."

Yorkshire singers do not in general start with the first verse. It is more usual to commence—

"'Tis true my love has listed,
He wears a white cockade."

Another set of the air is appended, which is thus arranged—

WHITE COCKADE.

(Second Version.)

'Tis true my love has list - ed, he wears a white cockade! He is a hand-some young man, be - side a ro - ving
blade; He is a hand-some young man, and he's gone to serve the
king: Oh, my ve - ry, Oh, my ve - ry, Oh, my ve - ry, Oh, n...
ve - ry, my ve - ry heart is break - ing all for the love of him.

POLLY OLIVER'S RAMBLE.

POLLY OLIVER is one of the numerous ballads or songs which narrate the adventures of a young lady who dons male attire to follow her true love. The song is an early one, and is found on ballad sheets. Chappell prints a very beautiful air, presumably from tradition, to which he unites, " Fair Hebe I left with a cautious design,"—an old song already fitted with a tune.

The two following airs are other settings of the song.

The first version I find in an old manuscript book of airs in my possession, and it is a tune well worth preservation. The second air is from a traditional source.

POLLY OLIVER'S RAMBLE.

One night Polly Oliver lay musing in bed,
A comical fancy came into her head :
Neither father nor mother shall make me false prove,
I'll list for a soldier and follow my love.

So early next morning this fair maid arose,
And dressed herself up in a suit of men's clothes ;
Coat, waistcoat, and breeches, and a sword by her side,
On her father's black gelding like a dragoon did ride.

She rode till she came into fair London town,
She dismounted her horse at the sign of the " Crown ;"
The first that came to her was a man from above,
The next that came down was Polly Oliver's true love.

" Good evening, good evening, kind Captain," said she,
" Here's a letter from your true love, Polly Oliver," said she ;
He opened the letter, and a guinea was found,
" For you and your companions to drink the health round."

. . . .

For the rest of Polly Oliver's adventures I must refer the reader
to the broadside copy of the song ; enough is here given to serve as
a vehicle for the airs.

The following second set of " Polly Oliver" I noted down from
the singing of Mr. Robert Holliday, of Newton-Dale, North
Yorkshire, where this version of the melody is best known.

POLLY OLIVER.

(Second Version.)

One night, as Pol-ly Ol-iv-er lay a mu - sing in bed, A

com - i - cal fan - cy came in - to her head: Nei-ther

fa - ther nor mo - ther shall make me false prove ; I'll

list and be a sol - dier, to fol-low my true love.

THE BONNY SCOTCH LAD.

THE air, which is pleasing, is from Mr. A. Wardill, of Goathland, who learned it from his grandfather's singing. Mr. Wardill is in possession of a copy of the words of the song written down by this relative about the years 1805-10.

The words are also found on broadsides, and a version of them, commencing—

"At Kingston-upon-Waldy, a town in Yorkshire,"

is in *A Pedlar's Pack of Ballads and Songs*, 1869. Another is in *Yorkshire Anthology*, edited by J. O. Halliwell, 1851; besides one in Ingledew's *Ballads and Songs of Yorkshire*, 1860.

The names of the town in these copies vary between Kingston-upon-Woolwich and Kingston-upon-Hull; the words, too, are all more or less different to the following from the manuscript above spoken of and here printed. It is almost identical with a broadside copy printed in Leeds.

THE BONNY SCOTCH LAD.

'Twas down in a val-ley near a town in York-shire, I lived at my
ease and was free from all care; I lived at my ease and had
sweet-hearts e-new, Till I met with a lad in his bon-net so blue.

'Twas down in a valley, near a town in Yorkshire,
I lived at my ease and was free from all care;
I lived at my ease and had sweethearts enew,
Till I met with a lad with his bonnet so blue.

A regiment of soldiers, as you shall soon hear,
From Scotland to Kingston came abroad for to steer ;
There was one lad amongst them, I loved him so true,
He's a bonny Scotch lad with his bonnet so blue.

His cheeks were like roses, his eyes like two sloes,
He's proper and handsome wherever he goes ;
Besides, he's good-natured, and comely to view,
He's a bonny Scotch lad with his bonnet so blue.

It was early one morning I rose from my bed,
I called for my Nelly, my own waiting-maid ;
"Come, dress me as well as your two hands can do,
I'm going to see the lads with their bonnets so blue."

When I came to the regiment it was on parade,
I listened intently to hear what was said ;
His name was Charles Stewart, I love him so true,
He's a bonny Scotch lad with his bonnet so blue.

My love he passed by with a gun in his hand,
I strove to speak to him, but it was all in vain,
I strove to speak to him, but by me he flew,
But my heart went along with his bonnet so blue.

I said, " My dear jewel, I'll buy your discharge
From the army, I'll free you and set you at large ;
If you can but love me, my heart will be true,
For well I do love your sweet bonnet so blue."

He says, " My fair lady, if you me discharge,
And free me from the army and set me at large ;
If I were to leave and along with you go,
It's what would my poor little Scotch lassie do ?

" For I've got a sweetheart in my own country,
I will never despise for her poverty ;
The girl that I love she'll always prove true,
And I'll ne'er put a stain on my bonnet so blue."

I'll send for a limner from London to Hull,
I'll have my love's picture drawn out at the full ;
And in my bedchamber so oft will I view,
My bonny Scotch lad with his bonnet so blue.

THE PLAINS OF WATERLOO.

SHORTLY after the Battle of Waterloo a ballad was much sung both in Scotland and in England, giving a narrative of the famous fight, and recording the names of the officers who fell or who distinguished themselves for their bravery.

I have come across at least three or four different versions of the ballad, and three airs for it. One of these airs is in Christie's *Traditional Ballad Airs*, but the two which I here print are quite dissimilar from it and from each other.

The first version I obtained from a country singer in Dumfries-shire, along with the better known copy of the ballad.

THE PLAINS OF WATERLOO.
(First Version.)

On the sixteenth day of June, my boys, In Flanders, where we lay, Our
bu-gles sound-ed the a-larm Be-fore the break of day; We
Bri-tons, Bel-gians, Bruns-wickers, and Han - o-ver - ians too,
All Brus-sels left that morn-ing For the plains near Wa-ter-loo.

On the sixteenth day of June, my boys, in Flanders where we lay,
Our bugles sounded the alarm before the break of day ;
We Britons, Belgians, Brunswickers, and Hanoverians too,
All Brussels left that morning for the plains near Waterloo.

By a forced march we did advance till three in the afternoon,
Each British heart with ardour beat to pull the tyrant down ;
Near Quatre-Bras we met the French, their shape to us seemed new,
For in steel armour they were clad on the plains of Waterloo.

Napoleon to his men did say before that they begun,
" My heroes, if we lose the day, our nation is undone ;
The Prussians we've already beat—we'll beat the British, too,
And display victorious eagles on the plains of Waterloo."
Etc. etc.

The above version of the ballad is said to be the composition of
a Sergeant Grant of the 92nd regiment, who wrote it directly after
the battle. As it is the copy most frequently met with on broadsides, and is reprinted in Logan's *Pedlars' Pack of Ballads*, and a
similar version is given by Christie, I have used the space at my
disposal in giving a less known copy of the ballad from a broadside.

A Horbury correspondent sends me the second setting of the
" Plains of Waterloo," as learned by his grandfather and himself
from Waterloo men ; he informing me that it was the tune preferred
and mostly sung by the Waterloo heroes. The music is set to the
third verse.

THE PLAINS OF WATERLOO.
(Second Version.)

On the eighteenth day of June, my boys, Eighteen hundred and fif-
teen, Both horse and foot they did advance, Most glorious to be
seen; Both horse and foot they did advance, And the bugle horn did
blow: The sons of France we made them dance On the plains of Water - loo.

The ancient sons of glory were all great men they say,
And we, in future story, will be as great as they ;
Our noble fathers' valiant sons shall conquer every foe,
And long shall fame their names proclaim, who fought at Waterloo.

At ten o'clock on Sunday, the bloody fight began,
In raged from that moment to the setting of the sun ;
My pen, I'm sure, can't half relate the glories of that day
We fought the French at Waterloo, and made them run away.

On the eighteenth of June, eighteen-hundred-and-fifteen,
Both horse and foot they did advance, most glorious to be seen,
Both horse and foot they did advance, and the bugle horn did blow,
The sons of France we made them dance, on the plains of Waterloo.

Our cavalry advanced with true and valiant hearts,
Our infantry and artillery did nobly play their parts ;
While the small arms did rattle and great guns did roar,
And many a valiant soldier lay bleeding in his gore.

The French dogs made a bold attack in front of Mount St. Jean,
Two of their best battalions thought the village to gain ;
Our infantry first charged them and made them face about,
Sir William with his heavy brigade soon put them to the rout.

As for Sir William Ponsonby, I'm sorry for to say,
Leading the Enniskillen dragoons, he met his fate that day ;
In front of his brigade he fell, which grieves me very sore,
I saw him lie as I passed by, with many thousands more.

The cuirassiers so nobly fought, armed in coats of steel,
And boldly they did advance, thinking to make us yield ;
But our dragoons with sword in hand soon cut their armour through,
And showed that day at Waterloo, what Britons they could do.

Napoleon, like a fighting cock, far mounted on a car,
He much did wish to represent great Mars the god of war ;
On a high platform he did stand and loudly he did crow,
He dropt his wings and turned his tail to us at Waterloo.

The fertile field of Brabant shall long recorded be,
Where Britons fought for honour and Belgic liberty,
The Sovereign of the Netherlands, he very well does know,
For honour and his country, we fought at Waterloo.

The Prince of Orange the hussars and right wing did command,
And sure a Prince more valiant ne'er took a sword in hand ;
His Highness wounded was that day, charging the haughty foe,
And long shall fame their name proclaim, who fought at Waterloo.

The valiant Duke of Brunswick fell in the field that day,
And many a valiant officer dropt in the awful fray,
And many British soldiers lay bleeding in their gore,
On the plains of Waterloo, where thundering cannons roar.   ·

Lord Wellington commanded us all on that glorious day,
Where many a brave soldier in death's cold arms did lay ;
Where many arms did rattle, and cannons loud did roar,
At Waterloo, where Frenchmen their fate did deplore.

As for General Paget, Marquis of Anglesea,
The commander of the brigade of British cavalry,
His honour most conspicuous shone wherever he did go,
A limb he lost in a gallant charge that day at Waterloo.

Brave General Hill, so much renowned, commanded the left wing,
And with his British hearts of oak, destruction did bring ;
Brave Picton of heroic fame his squadron on he drew,
Where sublime his deeds do shine in fame at Waterloo.

Now, tender husbands here have left their wives to mourn,
And children, weeping, cry, "When will our dads return?"
Our country will dry up their tears, we feel rejoiced to know,
They will reward each soldier that fought at Waterloo.

When Buonaparte he did perceive the victory we had won,
He did lament in bitter tears, saying, "Oh ! my darling son,
I will set off to Paris straight, and have him crowned also,
Before they hear of my defeat on the plains of Waterloo."

So unto George, our gracious King, my voice I mean to raise,
And to all gallant commanders I wish to sing their praise ;
The Duke of York and family, and Wellington also,
And the soldiers brave that fought that day on the plains of Waterloo.

So let us give our praise to God, who did the victory give,
And may we all remember Him as long as we do live ;
To God above give all the praise, and we'll remember, too,
That He gave to us the victory on the plains of Waterloo.

Another ballad on the "Plains of Waterloo" will be found
spoken of under the tune, "With Henry Hunt we'll go," in the
present volume.

—+•+—

BRENNAN ON THE MOOR.

I HAVE not sought out from the criminal records a history of
the Irish highwayman, Willie Brennan. Judging by the popularity of the song, he must have been somewhat famous, and he
appears to have excited the sympathy of the crowd. The song is or
was sung all over England, and it is common on ballad sheets. I

have not met with more than one air to it, and that was picked up in two halves. Some copies of the ballad speak of the "Livart" and "Lilvart mountains," instead of the "Limerick mountains."

BOLD BRENNAN ON THE MOOR.

It's of a fear-less high-way-man a sto-ry now I'll tell: His name was Wil-lie Brennan, and in Ire-land he did dwell; 'Twas on the Limerick mountains he com-menced his wild career, Where many a wealthy gen-tle-man be-fore him shook with fear. Brennan on the moor, Brennan on the moor, Bold and yet un-daunt-ed stood young Brennan on the moor.

It's of a fearless highwayman a story now I'll tell :
His name was Willie Brennan, and in Ireland he did dwell ;
'Twas on the Limerick mountains he commenced his wild career,
Where many a wealthy gentleman before him shook with fear.

CHORUS.
Brennan on the moor, Brennan on the moor,
Bold and yet undaunted stood young Brennan on the moor.

A brace of loaded pistols he carried night and day,
He never robb'd a poor man upon the King's highway ;
But what he'd taken from the rich, like Turpin and Black Bess,
He always did divide it with the widow in distress.

One night he robbed a packman, his name was Hedler Bawn* ;
They travelled on together, till day began to dawn ;
The pedlar seeing his money gone, likewise his watch and chain,
He at once encountered Brennan and robbed him back again.

When Brennan saw the pedlar was as good a man as he,
He took him on the highway, his companion for to be ;
The pedlar threw away his pack without any more delay,
And proved a faithful comrade until his dying day.

One day upon the highway Willie he sat down,
He met the Mayor of Cashel, a mile outside the town ;
The Mayor he knew his features, " I think, young man," said he,
" Your name is Willie Brennan, you must come along with me."

As Brennan's wife had gone to town provisions for to buy,
When she saw her Willie, she began to weep and cry ;
He says, " Give me that tenpence ;" as soon as Willie spoke,
She handed him the blunderbuss from underneath her cloak.

Then with his loaded blunderbuss, the truth I will unfold,
He made the Mayor to tremble, and robbed him of his gold ;
One hundred pounds was offered for his apprehension there,
And with his horse and saddle to the mountains did repair.

Then Brennan being an outlaw upon the mountain high,
Where cavalry and infantry to take him they did try,
He laughed at them with scorn, until at length, it's said,
By a false-hearted young man he was basely betrayed.

In the County of Tipperary, in a place they call Clonmore,
Willie Brennan and his comrade that day did suffer sore ;
He lay among the fern which was thick upon the field,
And nine wounds he had received before that he did yield.

Then Brennan and his companion knowing they were betrayed,
He with the mounted cavalry a noble battle made ;
He lost his foremost finger, which was shot off by a ball ;
So Brennan and his comrade they were taken after all.

So they were taken prisoners, in irons they were bound,
And conveyed to Clonmel jail, strong walls did them surround ;
They were tried and found guilty, the judge made this reply,
" For robbing on the King's highway you are both condemned to die,'

* In some copies, "Pedlar Brown."

Farewell unto my wife, and to my children three,
Likewise my aged father, he may shed tears for me,
And to my loving mother, who tore her gray locks and cried,
Saying, " I wish, Willie Brennan, in your cradle you had died."

SPENCE BROUGHTON.

SPENCE BROUGHTON was a Sheffield man who robbed the Rotherham postman on Attercliffe Common, and was executed for this crime at York, on the 14th of April, 1792. His body was hung on a gibbet near the scene of the robbery, the gibbet-post remaining standing till 1827. Although but few singers know much about Spence Broughton, and though the song is far from being good, it appears to have lingered in South Yorkshire to our own time—a hundred years after its composition.

I have obtained two copies of the air. The words are on broadsides printed at Leeds.

SPENCE BROUGHTON.

To you, my dear companions, Accept these lines I pray: A
most impartial trial . . Has oc-cu-pied this day; 'Tis
from your dying Brough-ton, To show his wretched fate: Pray,
make your re-form-ation . . Be-fore it is too late.

To you, my dear companions, accept these lines, I pray:
A most impartial trial has occupied this day ;
'Tis from your dying Broughton, to show his wretched fate
Pray, make your reformation before it is too late.

The loss of your companion will grieve your hearts full sore,
I know that my fair Ellen will my wretched fate deplore ;
Thinking of those happy hours that now are past and gone,
That I, unhappy Broughton, would I had ne'er been born.

. . . .

Brought up in wicked habits, which wrought in me no fear,
How little did I think that my time had been so near ;
But now I am overtaken, I am bound and cast to die,
Exposed a sad example to all that does pass by.

O, that I had but gone unto some far distant clime,
Then a gibbet post for Broughton would never have been mine ;
But as for such like wishes, they are vanity and vain,
Alas ! it is but folly and madness to complain.

One night to try and slumber I closed my weeping eyes,
I heard a foot approaching, which struck me with surprise ;
I listened for a moment, a voice made this reply,
" Prepare thyself, Spence Broughton, to-morrow thou must die."

. . . .

Farewell, my wife and children, to you I bid adieu,
I never should have come to this had I stayed at home with you ;
But I hope through my Redeemer to gain a happy shore,
Farewell, farewell for ever, Spence Broughton is no more.

The following is the second and a better version of the air :—

SPENCE BROUGHTON.

(Second Version.)

To you, my dear com - pan - i - ons, Ac - cept these lines I pray : A

most im - par - tial tri - al Has oc - cu - pied this day : 'Tis

from your dy - ing Broughton, To show his wretched fate : Pray

make you re - for - ma - tion Be - fore it is too late.

THE EXECUTION SONG.

IN the palmy days of street singing, ballad-mongers quickly seized the golden opportunity of an execution for the production of a "last dying speech and confession;" which hawked and sung about the streets produced a plentiful harvest of pennies. Like certain enterprising newspapers in the same case, the ballad publisher had the account of the criminal's death in print long before the sentence of the law was carried out, for it was necessary to cater to the public before its morbid curiosity was worn off.

It will be seen also that a ready-made air was essential, and the following was the one to which nearly all this dismal class of songs were sung.

An attentive examination of the tune will, I think, show that when rid of the nasal twang imparted by the street singers to it, and, when put to better words, it is a fine air. I am in the first instance obliged to Mr. Holgate, of Leeds, for the remembrance of it, though to most of the older natives of Leeds it produces a recollection of a street singer with a Cockney accent, singing through his nose, such a song as I print to the air.

The refrain was judiciously varied; it was either—

> "Parents all, far and near,
> Listen now to what you hear."

or else—

> "Young men all now beware,
> Lest you fall into a snare."

according to the nature of the case.

A good story is told of a man who, being very hard up, conceived this happy notion of getting a few stray coppers:—An execution had occurred that same morning, and it now being a dark night, the man got from a grocer several sheets of blank tea paper, and proceeded to cry, "The last dying speech and confession of——, who was executed this morning at——," etc. etc.

Many people came running out or sent their children for the purchase of this latest intelligence, but they were woefully deceived on discovering they had given a penny for a piece of blank tea paper. The ingenious vendor was soon overtaken in another street however. "How's this, mister? there's nowt on this." "Why," said the man, "he said nowt."

The following ballad is a very typical specimen of the execution songs and is from a broadside :—

AWFUL EXECUTION OF JOHN BIRD BELL.

Ye pa-rents who have ten-der hearts, I pray you lend an ear, Of a

lit-tle boy, six-teen years old, A mourn-ful tale you'll hear: Con-

demned of late for a murd'rous crime, Thro' his pa-rents' guilt you see, You'd

weep and cry to see him die up-on the gal-low's tree; Pa-rents

all, far and near, Lis-ten now to what you hear.

"Awful execution of John Bird Bell, a boy aged 16 **years,** for the murder of Richard Taylor, aged 13, at Maidstone, **on** Saturday last."

[Here follows a prose account of the murder.]

> Ye parents who have tender hearts,
> I pray you lend an ear,
> Of a little boy, sixteen years old,
> A mournful tale you'll hear:

Condemned of late for a murd'rous crime,
 Thro' his parents' guilt you see,
You'd weep and cry to see him die
 Upon the gallows tree.
  Parents all, far and near,
  Listen now to what you hear.

When he was sentenced at the bar,
 The court was drowned in tears,
To see a boy so young cut off
 All in his infant years.
Such piercing cries his mother made,
 Her gray hairs she did tear,
And loud and long she did lament .
 When his sentence she did hear.
  Parents all, far and near,
  Listen now to what you hear.

The hardest heart would melt in tears
 To hear the boy's sad moan ;
At the bar he screamed and trembled
 When his sentence was made known.
With pickpockets at fairs he then confessed
 His parents made him comply,
To join a mob to murder and rob,
 For which he's doomed to die.
  Parents all, far and near,
  Listen now to what you hear.

Religious thoughts he ne'er was taught,
 No church or prayer brought nigh ;
For want of parents' proper care,
 This boy's condemned to die.
  Parents all, far and near.
  Listen now to what you hear.

Another lugubrious ditty to this tune is, " The Downfall of Young Henry the Poacher," a narrative of the miseries of transportation to Van Dieman's Land.

YOUNG HENRY THE POACHER.

Come, all you wild and wicked youths, wherever you may be,
I pray you give attention and listen unto me ;
The fate of us poor transports, as you shall understand,
The hardships that we undergo upon Van Dieman's Land.
 Young men all now beware,
 Lest you're drawn into a snare, etc.

THE DEATH OF BILL BROWN

"BILL BROWN" is a poaching song, having some popularity in Yorkshire. There are two separate songs which sing the unhappy death of this individual who was a poacher shot by a gamekeeper at a village named Brightside, near Sheffield. This was so long ago as 1769, and it is most extraordinary that the narrative of this circumstance should have existed for so many years in traditional song, for the verses which record it are found reprinted on ballad sheets up to nearly the present day.

The version of the tune I here print is the one best known; it has been noted down for me by Mr. Lolley, at Goole, and I also find from another correspondent that it is identical with the set sung in the Leeds district. The words of the ballad I have reprinted from a broadside.

BILL BROWN.

Ye gentlemen, both great and small,
Gamekeepers, poachers, sportsmen all,
Come, listen to a simple clown,
I'll sing you the death of poor Bill Brown,
I'll sing you the death of poor Bill Brown :

One stormy night, as you shall hear
(It was in the season of the year),
We went to the woods to catch a fat buck,
But, ah ! that night we had bad luck—
Bill Brown was shot and his dog was stuck.

When we got to the woods, our sport begun,
I saw the gamekeeper present his gun ;
I call'd on Bill to climb the gate,
To fetch the fat buck, but it was too late,
For there he met his untimely fate.

Then, dying he lay upon the ground,
And in that state poor Bill I found ;
And when he saw me he did cry,
" Revenge my death ;" " I will," said I,
" For many a hare we have caught hard by."

I know the man that shot Bill Brown,
I know him well and could tell the clown ;
And to describe it in my song—
Black jacket he had, and red waistcoat on,
I know him well, and they call him Tom.

I dressed myself up next night in time,
I got to the wood, and the clock struck nine ;
The reason was, and I'll tell you why,
To find the gamekeeper I'll go try,
Who shot my friend, and he should die.

I ranged the wood all over, and then
I looked at my watch and it was just ten ;
I heard a footstep on the green,
I laid myself down for fear of being seen,
For I plainly saw that it was Tom Green.

Then I took my piece fast in my hand,
Resolved to fire if Tom did stand ;
Tom heard the noise and turned him round,
I fired and brought him to the ground—
My hand gave him his deep death wound.

Now revenge, you see, my hopes have crowned,
I've shot the man that shot Bill Brown ;
Poor Bill no more these eyes will see—
Farewell, dear friend, farewell to ye,
For I've crowned his hopes and his memory.

Another version of the ballad of "Bill Brown," which I have not been able to obtain the air for, is found on a broadside printed by Harkness, of Preston. It gives a more detailed account of the fray; and whatever air it may be now sung to, it appears to have originally been adapted to the old Scotch tune, "The Mill, Mill, O." One verse is here appended:—

> In seventeen hundred and sixty-nine,
>   As plainly doth appear, then,
> A bloody scene was felt most keen,
>   Till death it did draw near, then.
> Of poor Bill Brown, of Brightside town,
>   A lad of well-known fame, then,
> Who took delight both day and night,
>   To trace the timid hare, then.

. . . .

HARES IN THE OLD PLANTATION.

IN country places where poaching is, among a certain class of people, considered rather as a virtue than a crime, songs descriptive of the delights of that illicit sport abound. The only poaching song that has attained anything like a station in respectable society is, "It's my delight on a shiny night," which commences—

"When I was bound apprentice in famous Lincolnshire,"

and this is due more to the merit of the air rather than that of the words, and from the fact that it was a favourite of George IV. To this same tune of the "Lincolnshire Poacher," is sung a favourite Yorkshire poaching song, "The Sledmere Poachers."

> Come, all ye gallant poaching lads, and gang along with me,
> And let's away to Sledmere woods some game for to see ;
> It's far and near, and what they say, it's more to feel than see,
> So come, my gallant poaching lads, and gang along with me.

Another poaching song started—

> Come, all you lads of high renown,
> That love to drink good ale that's brown,
> That pull the lofty pheasant down,
> With powder, shot, and gun, etc.

and another, "The Oakham Poachers," began in this dismal strain—

> Young men, in every station,
> That live within this nation,
> Pray, here my lamentation—
> A solemn, mournful tale—
> Concerning three young men,
> That now do lie condemned,
> And heavy bound in irons,
> In Oakham county jail.

A fitting pendant to this is, "The Downfall of Young Henry the Poacher," a verse of which is given in the present volume on page 130.

"Hares in the Old Plantation" is a song originally consisting of a number of verses so deficient of rhyme and reason as to be not worth the trouble of transcription, though the air is by no means a bad one. The song was obtained for me at Goole.

HARES IN THE OLD PLANTATION.

My fa-ther turned me out of doors, I'd no home nor hab - i - ta - tion !

took my dog, my gun, and snares a - way to the old plan - ta - tion : I'll

ne - ver want a piece of bread while there's hares in the old plant-t-t-on.

> My father turned me out of doors,
> I'd no home nor habitation ;
> I took my dog, my gun, and snares,
> Away to the old plantation.
>> I'll never want a piece of bread,
>> While there's hares in the old plantation.

O then I crossed a field or two
Without any hesitation,
When up jump'd one, and away she ran,
Away to the old plantation.
    Refrain—When up jump'd one, etc.

My dog he started after her,
Without any invitation ;
He caught her by the back so small,
Leaping in the old plantation.
    Refrain—He caught her by, etc.

. . . .

I went into a public-house,
On the table threw her down, sir,
"A brace of hares I'll give to thee,
If thou'll pay me a crown, sir."
    Refrain—A brace of hares, etc.

. . . .

———◆◆———

THE COCK FIGHT.

THE brutal sport of cock-fighting is happily now at an end. The
following song is a relic of the pastime, which I admit merely
for the sake of the air. The song used to be sung by ardent cock
fighters in and about Hunslet and Holbeck, two districts of Leeds,
and I have obtained several copies of the air and words. Holbeck
and Hunslet Moors were, forty years ago, the scene of many cock
battles. The patrons of the sport formed an extempore cock pit by
forming a ring round the arena : the first row sitting, the next row
kneeling, and the outer spectators standing. In this manner all
were enabled to see the combat, and if any unlucky individual in
the inner circle, in his eagerness to obtain a better view, stood up,
whack ! came a stick on his unlucky head from those whose view
he had hindered.

The air is rather remarkable for being somewhat similar to the
traditional version of "'The Bailiff's Daughter of Islington," first
published by Chappell, and it is more than likely that the cock-fight

verses have been adapted to the tune, "The Bailiff's Daughter," has been sung to in Leeds.

THE HOLBECK MOOR COCK-FIGHT.

Come, all ye Cock-ers, far and near! I'll tell you of a cock-fight, The
when and where On Holbeck Moor, as I've heard say, Between a black and a bon-ny grey.

> Come, all ye Cockers, far and near !
> I'll tell you of a cock-fight, the when and where,
> On Holbeck Moor, as I've heard say,
> Between a black and a bonny grey.
>
> Twelve men from Hunslet town they came,
> Along with them that brought their game ;
> This game it was, as I've heard say,
> Of a black to fight with a bonny grey.

Other verses follow which describe the incidents of the fight. The last verse is :—

> And when the clock struck one, two, three,
> The grey struck the black upon the thigh ;
> They picked him up to see fair play,
> But the black would not fight with the bonny grey.

In explanation of the last two lines, it may be stated that if one of the birds turned tail it was held as a sign of cowardice, and by the rules of cocking both birds were then taken up from the ground by those who fought them. The cock that had turned tail was then put on the ground, and if he attacked the other bird, situated as he was held above him in the man's arms, the fight was allowed to proceed ; but if not, he was considered vanquished.

Strictly speaking, this perhaps should be called the Hunslet Moor Cock Fight, as the game was much more prevalent in Hunslet than Holbeck ; besides, Hunslet had a church clock, and Holbeck having only at that time a chapel, had no public clock.

The rhymes of "near" with "where," and of "three" with "thigh," may appear strange to those who do not know the dialect, but they are perfect as pronounced in the district.

THE FYLINGDALE FOX HUNT.

NEARLY every district has its hunting song, and the following is the one popular in the moorland parish of Fylingdales, to the south of Whitby.

It is sung with great gusto and loud voice in little publichouses by sporting farmers.

FOX-HUNTER'S SONG.

Ye loy - al fox - hunt - ers, at - tend to my song: I'll sing of a fox - hunt. and not keep you long; In eigh - teen e- le - ven, the date of the year The four - teenth of Feb-r'y, as plain doth ap - pear, When the hills and the val-leys did oft-times e- cho, And re-spond to the sound of a loud tal - ly ho!

Ye loyal fox hunters, attend to my song,
If you'll give your attention I'll not keep you long ;
In eighteen eleven, the date of the year,
The fourteenth of Feb'ry, as soon doth appear,
When the hills and the valleys did oft times echo,
And respond to the sound of a loud "Tally-ho !"

In Fylingdale parish, near to Ramsdale Mill,
Bold reynard was headed all up a steep hill;
There were many employed in cutting the rocks,
But they threw down their tools and they followed the fox,
While the hills and the valleys did oft-times echo,
And resound to " Hark, forward ! Tally-ho! Tally-ho !"

. . . .

I have no wish to inflict upon the readers more than two verses
of this effusion.   Like all the songs of its class, it runs to about
twenty verses, and the prowess of every fox-hunting squire and
yeoman of the district is chronicled; highly interesting to those
who know the descendants of the persons mentioned, but rather
monotonous to the general reader.

The adjoining parish of Goathland, jealous of the fame of the
Fylingdale song, some thirty or forty years ago produced one to the
same air.

Now, it's all you brave sportsmen I pray you draw near,
If you'll listen to me your spirits I'll cheer,
For a day of hunting I'd have you enjoy,
In Goathland parish, with a loud Tally-ho !
    Where the hills and the valleys, etc.

There's John Brockett the huntsman, he rides like a man,
Likewise William Dowson as fast as he can ;
And all of the sportsmen are galloping so true,
Expecting bold reynard they'll very soon view.
    When the hills and the valleys, etc.
        Etc. etc.

The air is a good one, and sounds well sung by a few well-tuned
and lusty voices.   It is originally one of the numerous tunes to the
songs which have a *Derry Down* refrain, but is not a published
one.

The old favourite, " The Yorkshire Horsedealers," among others
is sung to a version of this air in North Yorkshire.

THE WHITE HARE.

A TUNE obtained for me by Mr. Lolley, from the singing of a man near Howden, now lately dead. Musicians will, I think, congratulate Mr. Lolley upon obtaining such a fine and sterling old air. I wish I could say as much for the words. I am informed that, many years ago several people round about Howden used to sing the song after a coursing match, but it is, I believe, now generally forgotten.

The words I find upon ballad sheets. The first line is either, " Near Maxwell town," or, " Near Mansfield town," but the Howden people always gave the name of the place as that of their own.

THE WHITE HARE.

Near Howden town, near Howden town, as I have heard them tell, There once was a white hare who used there to dwell; She's been hunt - ed by grey-hounds and bea - gles so fair, But ne'er a one ' a-mongst them could come near this white hare; With my fol de dol de rol de dol de lol de dol de lay!

Near Howden town, near Howden town, as I have heard them tell
There once was a white hare who used there to dwell ;
She's been hunted by greyhounds and beagles so fair,
But ne'er a one amongst them could come near this white hare.
  With my fol de dol, etc.

When they came to the place where this white hare used to lie,
They uncoupled the beagles and began for to try ;
They uncoupled the beagles and beat the brush around,
But never a white hare in that field was to be found.

It's Jemmy the huntsman and Tom the whipper-in,
Go look in yonder fernside and see if she be in ;
With that she took a jump, boys, and fast away she ran,
" It's yonder she is going, don't you see her, gentlemen?"

The footmen they did run and the huntsmen they did ride,
Such halloing and shouting there was on every side ;
Such halloing and shouting I ne'er before did know,
As though she had been running all the time through.

The horsemen and the footmen they all drew nigh,
Thinking that the white hare was going for to die ;
She slipt out of the bush and thought to run away,
But cruel were the beagles that caused her to stay.

'Twas twenty good beagles that caused her to die,
There was not one amongst them above a foot high ;
The number of dogs there's not to be found,
Nor ever better hunting upon the English ground.

SADDLE TO RAGS.

THIS ballad appears to have been very popular in the days when highwaymen were a feature in the travels of our ancestors. A different copy of the song is to be found in Dixon's *Early Ballads illustrative of History, Tradition, and Customs,* 1856, and previously it was contributed to a volume, issued ten years before, by the Percy Society. Mr. Dixon remarks on its popularity, and mentions that he took it down from the singing of a Yorkshire yeoman. It is, according to Mr. Dixon, to be sung to an air in the *Beggars' Opera,* " How happy could I be with either," originally a country dance tune named "The Rant," sometimes called "Give an ear to a frolicsome ditty."

The present version of the ballad is not Mr. Dixon's, but is taken from a scarce little song-book entitled, *The Manchester Songster*, 1792, there named, *The Yorkshire Farmer;* no air is attached.

The tune hereunder printed was obtained in the East Riding by Mr. Lolley.

SADDLE TO RAGS.

A song I will sing unto you, A song of a mer-ry in-tent: It is of a sil-ly old man That went to pay his rent, That went to pay his rent.

A song I will sing unto you—
A song of a merry intent ;
It is of a silly old man,
That went to pay his rent.

And as he was riding along—
A-riding along the highway—
A gentleman thief steps before the old man,
And thus unto him he did say :

" My friend, how dare you ride alone,
For so many thieves there now be,
If any should but light on you,
They'd rob you of all your money."

" If that they should light upon me,
I'm sure they'd be very ill-sped ;
For, to tell you the truth, my kind sir,
In my saddle my money I've hid."

So as they were riding along,
And going down a steep hill,
The gentleman thief slipped before the old man,
And quickly he bid him stand still.

The old man, however, being cunning,
  As in this world there are many ;
He threw the saddle right over the hedge,
  Saying, " Fetch it if thou wouldst have any."

The thief being so greedy of money,
  He thought that of it there'd been bags,
Whipt out a rusty old sword,
  And chopped the saddle to rags.

The old man put his foot in the stirrup,
  And presently he got astride,
He put the thief's horse to the gallop,
  You need not bid the old man ride.

" Nay, stay ! nay, stay !" says the thief,
  "And half the money thou shalt have ;"
" Nay, by my troth," says the old man,
  " For once I have cheated a knave."

And so the old man rode along,
  And went with a merry devotion,
Saying, " If ever I live to get home,
  T'will enlarge my daughter's portion."

And having arrived at home,
  And got there with merry intent ;
Says he, " Landlord, show me a room,
  And I'll pay you your half-year's rent."

They opened the thief's portmanteau,
  And from it they took out so bold,
A hundred pounds in silver,
  And a hundred pounds in gold.

The story of a highwayman being outwitted in this fashion has
often been told in prose and in verse.   Albert Smith in his novel,
Christopher Tadpole, tells the tale as, " How the Jolly Man got
Robbed."

YOUNG BUCKS A-HUNTING GO.

FOR the following very musical hunting song I am indebted to
Mr. Thomas Hewson, of Roundhay. It was, he informs
me, commonly sung on the borders of Staffordshire, Cheshire, and
Shropshire, between 1820 and 1840. The version of the song and
air is here given as it was sung by a follower of the Cheshire hounds
during that period.

BUCKS A-HUNTING GO.

How sweet is the horn that blows in the morn,
    Young bucks a-hunting go ;
How sweet is the horn that blows in the morn,
    Young bucks a-hunting go,
    Young bucks a-hunting go ;
All my fancy dwells upon Nancy,
    While I sing Tally-ho !

The fox leaped over the hedges so high,
    The hounds all after him go ;
The fox leaped over the hedges so high,
    The hounds all after him go,
    The hounds all after him go ;
All my fancy dwells upon Nancy,
    While I sing Tally-ho !

How sweet is my home, my low, little cot,
    Let my station be high or low ;
How sweet is my home, my low, little cot,
    Let my station be high or low,
    Let my station be high or low ;
All my fancy dwells upon Nancy,
    While I sing Tally-ho !

I have found a version of the above song printed in two editions
of a chap-book of songs, *circa* 1800, entitled, *The Royal Sportsman's
Delight*, one printed by T. Evans, Smithfield, London, and the
other by Pitts' Seven Dials.   It is as under :—

BUCKS A-HUNTING GO.

With hound and horn each rosy morn,
    Let bucks a-hunting go,
    Let bucks a-hunting go,
While all my fancy dwells upon Nancy,
    And her sweet Tally-ho !

Was she my wife, how sweet the life
    In station high or low,
    In station high or low,
'Midst wars alarms her music charms,
    And her sweet Tally-ho !

On heath or warren though near to barren,
    With her 'twould fruitful grow,
    With her 'twould fruitful grow,
Make violets spring, all verdure bring,
    When she sings Tally-ho !

The stag flies over the plain so fleet,
The hunters after him go,
The hunters after him go ;
No more they'll run, their sport be done,
If she sings Tally-ho !

The music of her voice, I'm sure,
Would charm poor Reynard's woe,
Would charm poor Reynard's woe ;
The chase would cease and all be peace,
If she sung Tally-ho !

So let's toast her health so free, my boys,
Ere home that we do go,
Ere home that we do go ;
On May day seen, my girl is queen
When she sings Tally-ho !

THE PRETTY PLOUGHBOY.

T HIS exceedingly sweet measure I took down from the singing
of a ploughman in North Yorkshire. The words are a
Yorkshire version of a song contained in Cromek's *Reliques of
Robert Burns,* 1808, but which may have been an older song touched
up by the poet. I have not been able to find any air for Burns' song
in the early Scottish musical publications. The air which I have
noted down from the Yorkshire singer is, I think, old and very
beautiful.

THE PRETTY PLOUGHBOY.

As I was a walk-ing one morn - ing in Spring, I

heard a pretty ploughboy, and so sweetly he did sing; And as he was a singing, oh ! these

words I heard him say, "There's no life like the ploughboy's in the sweet month of May."

As I was a-walking one morning in Spring,
I heard a pretty ploughboy, and so sweetly he did sing ;
And as he was a-singing, O ! these words I heard him say,
"There's no life like the ploughboy's in the sweet month of May.

"There's the lark in the morning, she will rise up from her nest,
And she'll mount the white air with the dew on all her breast,
And with this pretty ploughboy, O ! she'll whistle and she'll sing,
And at night she'll return to her nest back again."

.   .   .   .

THE ROVING HECKLER LAD.

IN the days of handloom weaving, a "Heckler," or "Hackler,"
was a man who heckled flax to make it ready for the distaff or
spinning wheel. It was a labour which required some degree of
exertion and skill, and therefore a heckler would, to ply his trade,
travel from village to village to heckle the flax which many house-
holders who had suitable land would grow themselves. The process
of heckling was carried on thus : a series of hackle pins, which are
stout steel points the size of darning needles, were fixed upright on
a board in front of the heckler, who flung the mass of flax upon
them, drawing it then towards him through the pins, so that, by
this method, the fibres of the mass were separated.

The hecklers were famous for wearing a fancy linen apron with
an ornamental fringe hanging from it. The wandering heckler is,
however, now a thing of the past, and his trade is superseded by
machinery; but the above account is from the remembrance of a
person who knew the time when the hecklers travelled about from
place to place as described.

The song of "The Roving Heckler Lad," used to be popular in
the clothing districts round about Leeds.

For the copy of the air I am indebted to Mr. Holgate.

THE ROVING HECKLER LAD.

I am a ro-ving Heck-ler lad, Through all the coun-try side I go; I tra-vel the world all o-ver, And earn my liv-ing so!

I am a roving heckler lad,
And by my trade I go ;
I travel the world all over
And get my living so.

The last verse finishes with :—

Here's a health to all good heckler lads,
In the room that my love's in.

The air has some degree of resemblance to the old ballad air, "Lord Thomas and Fair Eleanor," on page 40 of the present volume.

I AM A ROVER.

THE first version is another excellent air from Mr. Holgate's store of remembrance of Yorkshire song.

The words are found on broadsides, and copies differ slightly from each other.

I AM A ROVER.

I am a ro-ver, and that's well known; I am about to leave my home: Leav-ing my friends and my dear to mourn My bon-ny las-sie till I re-turn.

I am a rover, and that's well known,
I am about for to leave my home ;
Leaving my friends and my dear to mourn,
My bonny lassie till I return.

She drew a chair, and bade me sit down,
And soon she told me her heart I'd won ;
She turned her head when I took my leave,
" Farewell, my bonny lass, for me don't grieve."

I sat me down for to write a song,
I wrote it wide and I wrote it long ;
At every verse I shed a tear,
At every line, I cried, " My dear !"

"O, am I bound or am I free?
Or am I bound to marry thee?
A married life you soon shall see,
A contented mind is no jealousy."

As I crossed over Dannamore,*
There I lost sight of my true love's door ;
My heart did ache, my eyes went blind,
As I thought of the bonny lass I'd left behind.

" I wish, I wish, but it's all in vain,
I wish that he would return again ;
Return, return, he'll return no more,
For he died on the seas where the billows roar."

The second version of the air, which appears to be older in date,
has been communicated by Mr. Lolley from another part of Yorkshire.

The first line commences—

    " I am a roamer and that's well known."

I AM A ROVER.

(Second Version.)

I am a roam-er, and that's well known; I am a-bout to leave my home ; Leav-ing my friends and my dear to mourn, My bon-ny lass, till I re turn.

* In some copies, " Yon deary moor."

DOWN IN OUR VILLAGE.

" DOWN in Our Village" is a rustic song still occasionally heard. There appear to be two airs for it: the one hereunder printed, and an air which is sung to "Barbara Allen," named in the present volume *Third Version*, to be found on page 38. The song is often named, "Little Fan." The words are printed on broadsides.

DOWN IN OUR VILLAGE.

When first I was a shepherd boy, Shall I for-get? no, ne-ver! My sim-ple song I sung with joy, In rus-tic strains so clev-er; When work was done, all clean and neat: From sowing, plough, or til-lage, I went where lads and lass-es meet, Down, down in our vil-lage.

When first I was a shepherd boy,
    Shall I forget? no, never!
My simple song I sung with joy,
    In rustic strains so clever;
When work was done, all clean and neat,
    From sowing, plough, and tillage,
I went where lads and lasses meet,
    Down, down in our village.

'Twas on the green, where they all danc'd,
    I first beheld my Fanny;
She looked so nice as she advanced—
    None half so well, not any;
Now, when next morn my work began
    At sowing, plough, or tillage,
I thought of none but little Fan,
    Down, down in our village.

My dad and mam cry, " Fie ! for shame !"
Then laugh and joke and jeer me ;
Think I so young am much to blame,
From Fanny want to tear me ;
But lads and lassies, dad and mam,
And sowing, plough, and tillage,
I'll give up all for little Fan,
Down, down in our village.

But I don't mean to leave my home,
For Fanny yet to marry ;
Till money we've both sav'd a sum,
We are resolved to tarry ;
And then the village bells shall ring,
No sowing, plough, or tillage ;
Then Fan shall dance, and I will sing,
Down, down in our village.

BROCKLESBY FAIR

"BROCKLESBY FAIR" is sung in the East Riding of Yorkshire, as well as in Lincolnshire, where Brocklesby is
situated. The air was noted down at Howden. In a broadside it
is "Birmingham Fair," and no doubt the name is altered according
to the locality in which the song obtains favour.

BROCKLESBY FAIR.

As I was a go-ing to Brock-les-by fair, With my
fine scar-let coat and ev-ery-thing rare, Enough to en-tice lass-es
bux-om and gay Who are will-ing to go with young Ram-ble a - way!

As I was a going to Brocklesby fair,
With my fine scarlet coat and everything rare ;
Enough to entice lasses buxom and gay,
Who are willing to go with young Ramble away.

. . . .

Six other verses follow.

DOWN BY THE DERWENT SIDE.

THE river Derwent here alluded to is a small river which flows into the Ouse near Goole, and in this district the song is sometimes sung. It appears on broadsides, however, as "Shannon Side," and may be another instance of the alteration of the locality to suit local singers.

Two verses of the ballad must suffice. An air for it is to be found in Christie's *Traditional Ballad Airs*, but it is totally distinct from the following. It may be premised that, locally, "Derwent side" is pronounced "Darrant side."

DOWN BY THE DERWENT SIDE.

'Twas in the month of A - pril, One morn-ing, at the dawn, I met a love - ly dam - sel, A trip - ping o'er the lawn. "Where are you going to, sweet - heart?" She un - to me re-plied, "I'm going to seek my fa - ther's sheep Down by the Der - went side!"

'Twas in the month of April, one morning at the dawn,
I met a lovely damsel a-tripping o'er the lawn ;
"Where are you going to, sweetheart?" she unto me replied,
"I'm going to seek my father's sheep down by the Derwent side.'

I said, " My pretty maid, I'll bear you company,
If you have no objections that I should go with thee ;"
She said, " Kind sir, excuse me, my parents would me chide,
If I am seen with any man down by the Derwent side."

. . . .

THE BONNY IRISH BOY.

"THE Bonny Irish Boy" is from the singing of a Scotch girl.
The words are also found on a ballad sheet. I have not
thought it worth while to reprint the whole of the verses.

THE BONNY IRISH BOY.

When first that I was court-ed by a bon-ny Ir-ish boy, He
call-ed me his jew-el, his heart's de-light and joy.
It was in Dub-lin ci-ty, that place of no-ted fame, When
first my bon-ny Ir-ish boy A court-ing to me came.

When first that I was courted by a bonny Irish boy,
He called me his jewel, his heart's delight and joy ;
It was in Dublin city, that place of noted fame,
When first my bonny Irish boy a courting to me came.

His cheeks they are like roses, his hair is a light brown,
His locks, in ringlets shining, o'er his shoulder all hung down,
His teeth as white as ivory, his eyes as black as sloes,
He breaks the hearts of all the girls wherever that he goes.

Long time I kept his company in hopes to be his bride,
But now he's gone and left me to cross the raging tide ;
I'm afraid some other fair maid my true love will enjoy,
While I am left lamenting for my bonny Irish boy.

. . . .

WHEN ADAM WAS FIRST CREATED.

MR. J. H. Dixon, in printing a version of this song in his "Songs of the Peasantry of England," mentions that he has had considerable trouble in procuring a copy of it, and says that it used in former days to be very popular with aged people resident in the North of England. I have procured a copy of the tune to which the song was sung, along with a fragment of the words, from Mr. John Briggs, of Leeds.

Dixon's version commences—

"Both sexes give ear to my fancy,"

but Mr. Briggs' copy begins as under :—

WHEN ADAM WAS FIRST CREATED.

When Adam was first cre - a - ted, And Lord of the u-ni-verse crown'd, His

hap-pi-ness was not com-ple - ted Un - til he an helpmate was found ; He'd

all things in food that were want-ing, To keep and support him thro' life ; He'd

hor-ses and fox - es for hunt - ing, Which some men love better than life.

When Adam was first created,
    And lord of the universe crown'd,
His happiness was not completed
    Until that an helpmate was found ;
He'd all things in food that were wanting
    To keep and support him in life ;
He'd horses and foxes for hunting,
    Which some men love better than wife.

He'd a garden so planted by nature,
    Man cannot produce in his life ;
But, yet, the all-wise, great Creator,
    Still saw that he wanted a wife ;
Then Adam he lay in a slumber,
    And there he lost part of his side,
And when he awoke, he with wonder
    Saw beside him a beautiful bride.

She wasn't made out of his head, sir,
    To triumphant be over man ;
And she from his feet was not taken,
    To be spurned and be trampled upon ;
But out of man's side she was taken,
    His companion and equal to be ;
But though they in one are united,
    The man must be stronger than she.

Other versions of the song are to be met with among country
singers.

SPENCER THE ROVER.

OLD songs abound with allusions to "rovers" and "wanderers,"
and "Spencer the Rover" has been, despite its terrible
doggrel, popular in many parts of Yorkshire. I have obtained
copies of the air from many sources, all having some slight variation,
but the following is apparently as genuine a set of the air as could
be obtained

The words are found on Yorkshire ballad sheets, and no doubt
they are the production of the aforesaid Spencer, some wandering
ballad singer, who has not been endowed with much poetical
genius.

SPENCER THE ROVER.

These words were com - po - sed by Spen - cer the Ro - ver, Who trav - el - led most parts of Great Bri - tain and Wales; He being much re - du - ced, which caused great con - fu - sion, And that was the rea - son that a ramb - ling he went.

These words were composed by Spencer the Rover,
  Who travelled most parts of Great Britain and Wales ;
He being much reduced, which caused great confusion,
  And that was the reason that a rambling he went.

In Yorkshire, near Rotherham, he being on his ramble,
  Being weary of travelling, he sat down to rest,
At the foot of yon mountain there runs a clear fountain,
  With bread and cold water he himself did refresh.

It tasted more sweet than the gold he had wasted,
  Sweeter than honey, and gave more content ;
Till the thoughts of his babies lamenting their father,
  Brought tears in his eyes and caused him to lament.

The night being approaching, to the woods he resorted,
  With woodbine and ivy his bed for to make ;
He dreamed about sighing, lamenting, and crying,
  Come home to your children and rambling forsake."

On the fifth of November, I've reason to remember,
  When first I arrived to my family and wife ;
She stood so surprised to see my arrival,
  To see such a stranger once more in her sight.

My children flocked round me with their prit-prattling story,
  With their prit-prattling story to drive away care ;
So we'll be united, like ants live together,
  Like bees in one hive contented we'll be.

Now, I am placed in my cottage contented,
   With primroses and woodbine hanging round my door ;
As happy as they that have plenty of riches,
   Contented I'll stay, and go rambling no more.

WHEN I WAS A MAID.

ALTHOUGH the air to this quaint rhyme smacks too much of
   a modern production once highly popular to be ancient ;
yet the song itself bears intrinsic evidence of being of a very old ditty.

The whole scheme of the song proclaims this, and the allusions
to shoes of "Spanish black" and to the rich girdle confirm it. I
obtained the song from Mr. A. Wardill, of Goathland, North
Yorkshire.

WHEN I WAS A MAID.

When I was a maid, a maid, a maid, and lived with my auld mi-ther at
hame, I'd meat and I'd drink and I'd fine claithing, and mo-ney I
want-ed nane; Oh, then! oh, then! I was a maid, and lived
with my auld mither at hame, I'd meat and I'd drink and I'd
fine claith-ing, and mo-ney I want-ed nane.

When I was a maid, a maid, a maid,
   And lived with my auld mither at hame,
I'd meat and I'd drink and I'd fine claithing,
   And money I wanted nane.

O, then !ĮO then ! I was a maid,
And¦lived with my auld mither at hame ;
I'd meat and I'd drink and I'd fine claithing,
And money I wanted nane.

My gown was made of the finest silk,
And flounced right down to the ground ;
The girdle that I wore round my waist,
Was sell't for a hundred pounds.
O, then ! O, then ! I was a maid, etc.

My stockings were made from the softest woo',
And gartered aboon the knee ;
My shoes were made of the Spanish black,
And they buckled right merrily.
O, then ! O, then ! I was a maid, etc.

A young man came a wooing me,
He askèd me to wed ;
I was so fond when he showed me t' ring,
That "Yes" was the word I said.

O, then ! O, then ! I was a wife,
And frae my auld mither taen,
I'd sorrow and grief all t' days of my life,
And money I never had nane.

My gown was made of the coarsest stuff,
And slitten right down to the hand ;
The girdle that I wore round my waist,
Was aye but a tarry band.
O, then ! O, then ! I was a wife, etc.

My stockings were made from the coarsest woo',
And patched wi' mony a clout ;
My shoes were made of the auld tan leather,
And my tears cam' blobbling out.
O, then ! O, then ! I was a wife, etc.

THE JOLLY SHILLING.

MANY people will remember the old nursery rhyme,
"The Jolly Shilling," of which this is a version. Mr.
Washington Teasdale supplies the song and air from an early re-
membrance of it.

THE JOLLY SHILLING.

I love a jolly shilling, I love a jolly shilling, I love a jolly shilling as
I love my life; A penny for to spend, A penny for to lend, And
ten-pence carry home to my wife, wife, wife; A pint nor a quart won't
grieve me, Nor false young girl deceive me: Here's to my
wife who will kiss me When I come roll-ing home.

I love a jolly shilling, I love a jolly shilling,
I love a jolly shilling as I love my life ;
A penny for to spend, a penny for to lend,
And tenpence carry home to my wife, wife, wife.

CHORUS.

A pint nor a quart won't grieve me,
Nor false, young girl deceive me ;
Here's to my wife, who will kiss me
When I come rolling home.

I love a jolly tenpence, I love a jolly tenpence,
   I love a jolly tenpence as I love my life ;
A penny for to spend, and a penny for to lend,
And eightpence carry home to my wife, wife, wife.
   A pint nor a quart, etc.

The song if sung throughout becomes monotonous, for, except in the diminution of the twopence, no change occurs in it. In the sequel the original shilling becomes a vanishing coin :

   " I'll carry nothing home to my wife."

AN OLD CARD PLAYING SONG.

I DON'T suppose the following to be very old, but it is quaint, has a good air, and appears to be an inedited song.

It has been obtained from Mr. Washington Teasdale, who learned it some twenty-five or thirty years ago in India. The song gives one the idea of being an extemporaneous drinking song, each member of the company contributing a rhyme as he drains off his glass, the chorus being sung by the whole party.

THE CARD SONG.

Oh ! the king will take the queen : but the queen will take the knave : And since we're all to-geth - er, boys, We'll have a jol-ly stave. Here's to you, Tom Brown, Here's to you, with all my heart ! We'll have an - o - ther glass, my boy, At least, be - fore we part : Here's to you, Tom Brown.

O, the king will take the queen, but the queen will take the knave ;
And since we're all together, boys, we'll have a merry stave—
        Here's to you, Tom Brown,

        Here's to you, with all my heart ;
        We'll have another glass, my boys,
        At least, before we part.
        Here's to you, Tom Brown.

The queen will take the knave, but the knave will take the ten ;
And since we're all together, boys, we'll keep it up like men—
        Here's to you, Tom Brown, etc.

The knave will take the ten, but the ten will take the nine ;
And since we're all together, boys, we'll drink the best of wine.
        Here's to you, Tom Brown, etc.
        Etc. etc.

As the verse-making is entirely dependent upon the singer, the reader will be able to readily supply the missing links.

It concludes—

The four will take the tray, but the tray will take the deuce ;
And since we're all together, boys, we'll never cry a truce.
        Here's to you, Tom Brown, etc.

The tray will take the deuce, but the ace will take them all ;
And since we're all together, boys, we won't go home at all.
        Here's to you, Tom Brown, etc.

A parody of the song is found in an early number of *Punch*.

It has been before printed, in the *Leeds Mercury Weekly Supplement*, in an article on "Old Tunes," contributed by myself.

WITH HENRY HUNT WE'LL GO.

I N 1819, just after the "Peterloo Riots," the song, "With Henry Hunt we'll go," was much sung in and about Manchester. Although I have met with several people who remember the song being sung, yet I cannot get a complete version of it. To Mr. James B. Shaw, of Cornbrook, Manchester, I am indebted for the air and the fragment forming the chorus, and the first verse of the song is supplied by "S.B."—a correspondent in the *Manchester City News.*

Henry Hunt is now forgotten, but he was one of an early band of reformers. He was born in Wiltshire in 1773, and it is said that (being an opulent farmer) he offered, during an invasion panic in 1801, the whole of his stock, worth about £20,000, to the Government if it were needed.

Having been fined and imprisoned for challenging Lord Bruce, his feelings turned towards radicalism, and in 1819 he became the hero of " Peterloo."

On the 16th of August of that year a mass meeting of radical reformers from many Lancashire towns assembled in St. Peter's Fields, Manchester. Henry Hunt and several other gentlemen were sitting in a barouche, upon the box of which was a female attired as the figure of liberty. Although the crowd appears to have been peaceable, yet the magistrates were so ill-advised as to attempt to seize Henry Hunt, and the military were sent to assist Joseph Nadin the constable in executing the warrant of arrest. All was confusion, and the military plunged with drawn swords into the mass of human beings before any were conscious of their danger. The deaths and injuries sustained by this charge were long remembered, and coming while the memory of Waterloo was still fresh, the disastrous occurrence was spoken of as "Peterloo." Henry Hunt was imprisoned for two and a half years for his part in the transaction.

About this time there was a song, "The Battle of Waterloo," popular, and to the tune of this the Henry Hunt song was written.

The first verse of the "Battle of Waterloo" is :—

> 'Twas on the eighteenth day of June,
>   Napoleon did advance ;
> The choicest troops that he could raise
>   Within the bounds of France ;
> Their glittering eagles shone around,
>   And proudly looked the foe ;
> But the British lion tore their wings
>   On the plains of Waterloo.

CHORUS.

> With Wellington we'll go, we'll go, with Wellington we'll go ;
> For Wellington commanded on the plains of Waterloo.
>   Etc. etc.

In more modern times the same lively air was set to a doggrel ballad, " How Five-and-Twenty Shillings are expended in a Week," of which this verse is a good example of the whole :—

> There's fourpence goes for milk and cream,
>   And one and twopence malt,
> Three halfpence goes for vinegar,
>   Twopence halfpenny salt ;
> A penny goes for mustard,·
>   Three halfpence goes for bread,
> And threepence went the other night
>   For half a baked sheep's head.

CHORUS.

> So she reckoned up and showed him,
>   And the answer gave complete,
> How five-and-twenty shillings　　　·
>   Were expended in a week.

In Bunting's Irish airs, 1840, there is a tune called "The Jolly Ploughboy," and this air Samuel Lover used for his song, "The Low-Backed Car." This tune appears to be the original of the present one here printed. Bunting's is in much slower time.

WITH HENRY HUNT WE'LL GO.

With Hen-ry Hunt we'll go, my boys, With Hen-ry Hunt we'll go ;   We'll

mount the cap of li - ber - ty   In spite of Na-din Joe.

'Twas on the sixteenth day of August,
    Eighteen hundred and nineteen,
A meeting held in Peter Street
    Was glorious to be seen ;
Joe Nadin and his big bull-dogs,
    Which you might plainly see,
And on the other side
    Stood the bloody cavalry.

CHORUS.

With Henry Hunt we'll go, my boys,
    With Henry Hunt we'll go ;
We'll mount the cap of liberty
    In spite of Nadin Joe.

LANCASHIRE MORRIS DANCE.

M R. James B. Shaw, of Cornbrook, Manchester, forwards me
the following dance air, which he informs me used to be
in great favour at Lancashire "Rush-bearings." I learn from
Mr. Shaw that during the last thirty years the old rush-cart pro-
cession has scarcely been seen at all in country districts, but

previous to that time the "rush-bearing" was an annual ceremony at many of the "wakes" (an annual autumn holiday), held at some of the villages in the outskirts of Manchester.

The melody of the dance varies slightly in form in different localities, but the version here printed was more particularly in use at Newton Heath, a district about three miles from the centre of Manchester, and now included within the city boundary.

The following words are said to have been sung to the first part of the ditty :—

> Morris dance is a very pretty tune,
> And I will dance in my new shoon ;
> Morris dance is a very pretty tune,
> And I will dance in my new shoon.
> My new shoon are not so good,
> But I would dance it if I could ;
> My new shoon are not so good,
> But I would dance it if I could.

LANCASHIRE MORRIS DANCE.

THE FOGGY DEW.

T HIS peculiar air is taken from a book of manuscript airs for the violin, noted down about 1825 by a Yorkshire performer. In the MS. no words are appended, but these are here supplied from a broadside.

The air is, I believe, old, and may be a minor set of an air in Bunting's *Ancient Music of Ireland*, 1840, under the same title.

THE FOGGY DEW.

What shepherd was like me so blest,
　To tend his fleecy care,
For welcome unto yonder hills,
　I freely did repair ;
'Twas on a bank of mossy turf
　Where purple violets grew :
'Twas there I sat to tend my flocks,
　Down among the foggy dew.

To view the beauties of yon wood,
　I climbed a lofty hill,
Where golden flowers adorn the grove,
　Close by a trickling rill ;
And when I near my cottage came,
　My lambs together drew,
I espied a maid with a milking pail,
　Down among the foggy dew.

With haste I flew, for well I knew
　The stile sweet Jenny pass'd,—
With nimble steps I quickly trac'd,
　Till I o'ertook the lass ;
I begged to bear her milking pail,
　But she persisted no :
" Indeed, kind sir, I cannot stay,
　Yonder stands my brindled cow.

" Down in the dale sweet ivy grows,
　'Tis there my mother dwells,
My father he's a husbandman,
　And toils o'er yonder hills ;
And I alone through frost and snow,
　A milking go, 'tis true,—
'Tis charity to pity me
　Among the foggy dew."

I said, " My dear, with me comply,
　To you I will be true ;
Neither frost nor snow shall harm you,
　Nor yet the foggy dew."
With that she smil'd, and soon complied,
　And straight to church we went ;
And now we live in harmony,
　In love and sweet content.

I have heard another song called " The Foggy Dew" sung in
North Yorkshire to a variation having Irish characteristics of " Ye
Banks and Braes." Robert Burns, in mentioning the air to which
he wrote his song, tells George Thomson that he has heard that
it had been sung among the old Irish people ; and it is possible the
air heard in Yorkshire may have been a traditional survival.

The first verse of the North Yorkshire "Foggy Dew" runs nearly as follows :—

> One night as I sat in my cot,
> And patient watch did keep,
> My true love came up to my door,
> And bitterly she did weep ;
> She wept, she mourned, she tore her hair,
> And cried, "What shall 1 do?
> I pray you take pity and shelter me,
> For fear of the foggy dew."

. . . .

THE SOLDIER'S DREAM.

THOMAS CAMPBELL wrote his beautiful poem early in the present century, and it had several musical settings adapted to it. The one by T. Attwood is that most frequently met with. The following simple and charming air I have never seen in print. Mr. Lolley sends it me from his mother's singing.

THE SOLDIER'S DREAM.

Our bu - gles sang truce: for the night cloud had lower'd, And the sen - ti - nel stars set their watch in the sky, And thousands had sunk on the ground over-power'd, The wea - ry to sleep, and the wound - ed to die.

Our bugles sang truce—for the night-cloud had lower'd,
   And the sentinel stars set their watch in the sky ;
And thousands had sunk on the ground overpower'd—
   The weary to sleep, and the wounded to die.

When reposing that night on my pallet of straw,
   By the wolf-scaring faggot that guarded the slain ;
At the dead of the night a sweet vision I saw,
   And thrice ere the morning I dreamt it again.

Methought from the battle-field's dreadful array,
   Far, far I had roam'd on a desolate track :
'Twas autumn—and sunshine arose on the way
   To the home of my fathers, that welcom'd me back.

I flew to the pleasant fields traversed so oft
   In life's morning march, when my bosom was young ;
I heard my own mountain goats bleating aloft,
   And knew the sweet strain that the corn-reapers sung.

Then pledg'd we the wine-cup, and fondly I swore,
   From my home and my weeping friends never to part ;
My little ones kiss'd me a thousand times o'er,
   And my wife sobb'd aloud in her fulness of heart.

Stay, stay with us—rest, thou art weary and worn ;
   And fain was their war-broken soldier to stay ;
But sorrow return'd with the dawning of morn,
   And the voice in my dreaming ear melted away.

THE STOLEN CHILD.

THE air was noted down in East Yorkshire by Mr. Lolley,
   a similar copy of the tune being also heard in the West
Riding. It is but seldom sung, though the tune is good, but
both it and the words are not earlier than the early portion of the
present century. The words are found in print on a broadside.

THE STOLEN CHILD.

A - lone on the hea-ther a fair child was stray - ing, Whose

in - no - cent features were brighten'd with joy, And as 'mid the flow-ers he

care - less was playing. My heart yearn'd with love, and I spoke to the boy.

"Young stran-ger, whence art thou?" his blue eyes up - turn - ing, He

answer'd, "My home is yon tent on the plain, And ere the eve closes I

must be re - turn - ing, Or they will not let me roam hi - ther a - gain.

Alone on the heather a fair child was straying,
  Whose innocent features were brighten'd with joy,
And as 'mid the flowers he careless was playing,
  My heart yearn'd with love, and I spoke to the boy.
"Young stranger, whence art thou?" his blue eyes upturning,
  He answer'd, "My home is yon tent on the plain,
And ere the eve closes I must be returning,
  Or they will not let me roam hither again."

"Do thy parents await thee?" He paused, and the gladness
  That mantled his brow was o'ershadowed in gloom :
"I saw them but once," and he added with sadness,
  "They tell me that both are asleep in the tomb ;
The gipsy was kind, but my mother was fonder,
  She sang me so softly to rest in her arms ;
But now she is gone, and her darling must wander,
  Though the soft words she whisper'd my bosom still warms.

" And soon will I seek them where both are reposing,
    And take my best flowers to plant by their side,
That summer when all her bright tints are enclosing,
    May bless the green turf with their beauty and pride."
He bounded away, as my tears were fast falling
    To think how the gipsy such love had beguiled ;
I saw him no more, but the sad tale recalling,
    I often remember the poor stolen child.

TIME TO REMEMBER THE POOR.

"TIME to Remember the Poor" is a great deal in advance of the usual street ballad, and the air is an excellent one. I claim no very great degree of antiquity for either song or tune,—perhaps the beginning of the century may be fixed upon as the period of their composition. The tune and some of the words were noted down for me by Mr. Lolley from an East Riding singer. The words are on broadsides.

TIME TO REMEMBER THE POOR.

Cold win - ter is come with its cold chilling breath, And the leaves are all gone from the trees, And all seems touch'd by the fin - ger of death, And the streams are be - gin-ning to freeze; When the young wan-ton lads o'er the ri - ver slide, When Flo - ra at-tends us no more, When in plen - ty you're sit-ting by a warm fire - side, That's the time to re - mem-ber the poor.

Cold winter is come with its cold chilling breath,
    And the leaves are all gone from the trees,
And all seems touch'd by the finger of death,
    And the streams are beginning to freeze ;
When the young wanton lads o'er the river slide,
    When Flora attends us no more ;
When in plenty you're sitting by a warm fireside,
    That's the time to remember the poor.

The cold feather'd snow will in plenty descend,
    And whiten the prospect around ;
The keen, cutting wind from the north will attend,
    And cover it over the ground ;
When the hills and the dales are all candied with white,
    And the rivers are froze on the shore ;
When the bright, twinkling stars they proclaim the cold night,
    That's the time to remember the poor.

The poor, timid hare through the woods may be traced,
    With her footsteps indented in snow,
When our lips and our fingers are dangling with cold,
    And the marksman a shooting doth go,
When the poor robin redbreast approaches your cot,
    And the icicles hang at the door,
And when your bowl smokes reviving and hot,
    That's the time to remember the poor.

The thaw shall ensue, and the waters increase,
    And the rivers vehemently grow,
The fish from oblivion obtains release,
    And in danger the travellers go ;
When your minds are annoyed by the wide swelling flood,
    And your bridges are useful no more,
When in plenty you enjoy everything that is good,
    Do you grumble to think on the poor?

The time will come when our Saviour on earth,
    All the world shall agree with one voice,
All nations unite to salute the blest morn,
    And the whole of the earth shall rejoice ;
When grim death is deprived of his killing sting,
    And the grave rules triumphant no more,
Saints, angels, and men Hallelujah shall sing,
    Then the rich must remember the poor.

APPENDIX.

Since the foregoing sheets have been printed off, I have received several different airs to the songs therein contained.

A different air for "The Outlandish Knight" (see page 26) has been communicated by Mr. Lolley.

THE OUTLANDISH KNIGHT.
(Second Version.)

An Out-land-ish knight from the North-lands came, And he came a-woo-ing to me; He promised he'd take me to the Northlands, And there he would marry me.

From Mr. A. Wardill, Goathland, I get a different version of "Scarborough Fair" (see page 42).

SCARBOROUGH FAIR.
(Second Version.)

"O where are you going?" "To Scar - bo - rough Fair!" Rue, pars - ley, rose - ma - ry, and thyme! "Re - mem - ber me to a lass who lives there: For once she was a true love of mine."

Another tune for the "Golden Glove" (see page 49) has been noted down from the singing of a person at Goole.

THE GOLDEN GLOVE.

(Third Version.)

A wealth - y young squire of Tam - worth, we hear, He court - ed a no - ble-man's daughter so fair; And for to mar - ry it was his in - tent: All friends and re - la - tions had given their con-sent.

Mr. Lolley gives me an East Riding tune for "The Banks of Sweet Dundee" (see page 53).

THE BANKS OF SWEET DUNDEE.

(Second Version.)

It's of a farm - er's daugh - ter so beau - ti - ful, I'm told; Her fa - ther died and left her five hun - dred pounds in gold. She liv - ed with her un - cle, the cause of all her woe, And this mai - den fair, as you shall hear, did prove his o - ver - throw.

From Mr. A. Wardill, of Goathland, I get another setting of the popular favourite, "The Farmer's Boy" (see page 63).

THE FARMER'S BOY.

(Fourth Version.)

The sun was sunk be - hind yon hill, A - cross yon drea - ry moor, When poor and lame a boy there came Up to a farm-er's door. "Can you tell me if here it be That I can find em - ploy? To plough and sow, to reap and mow, And be a farm - er's boy."

Finis

Jas. Strafford, Music and General Printer, 113, Briggate, Leeds.

Note.

IT is the Editor's intention at a future date to issue a Supplementary Volume of "Traditional Tunes." As there must be a great many old unprinted airs still current in country districts, he makes the request that such persons who are possessed of any of these fugitive melodies, and who are willing to impart them, would contribute to the intended volume.

The fullest acknowledgment of these favours would be given.

128, BURLEY ROAD,
LEEDS.